Fly Fishing the Striper Surf

Fly Fishing the Striper Surf

FRANK DAIGNAULT

BURFORD BOOKS

Printed in Canada.

10 9 8 7 6 5 4 3 2 1

Library of Congress Cataloging-in-Publication Data
Daignault, Frank, 1936-
    Fly fishing the striper surf / Frank Daignault.
        p. cm.
    ISBN 1-58080-120-X (pbk.)
1. Striped bass fishing. 2. Surf fishing. I. Title.
SH691.S7D342 2004
799.17'732—dc22
                    2003021626

Contents

1

Finding Stripers

The Search for Evidence

Efficient striper hunting uses all the resources at the observer's disposal. It is not enough to know that bass are around. You have to consider the source of your information. Many "fishermen" spout off about what is happening on the Striper Coast when they don't have a clue. Others, often those with valuable and authentic inside information, deny all knowledge, shrugging emptily so as not to alarm the multitudes. Still, if the competent observer has reliable sources, it is possible to find out about the fishing socially. Sometimes striper activity is so robust that it cannot be kept secret. When such blitzes manifest themselves—and many seasons they do not happen anywhere—history can be made. Each season is different, and even when a beach does explode there is no guarantee that it will do so again the next year.

BAIT

Midwatch hunts for stripers are often nothing more than searching for the quarry that appeals to linesides. It is very unusual for large quantities of baitfish to be on any beach or estuary without having lured predators. Even when they appear to be unmolested, the wise angling detective keeps an eye on the bait for the eventual assault. It is usually only a matter of time. Even if bass fail to materialize, it is probably only because they found more bait elsewhere, or found it elsewhere sooner. For that reason any located baitfish should be noted and the search continued to determine which cache is most promising.

Nevertheless, the trick in making observations is being certain of their accuracy. Often surfcasters determine that there is no bait when, in fact, it is just more difficult to detect because of conditions. Moreover, as many of us have seen in fresh water, there can be a

Locating stripers like this one with my wife, Joyce, is a fine art that calls for close attention.

"masking" of the actual bait if you misidentify the forage. For instance, you could know that there are grass shrimp in your fore without realizing that bass are swilling on cinder worms. Usually it doesn't matter, but you can never have too much information when making a fly selection. The therapist's office is full of fly fishermen who thought they knew what the bass were eating.

Always stay attuned to available baitfish. Know what species are around and roughly the quantity of that bait to determine if you think this might appeal enough to bass to either attract or hold them. Fly choice begins with what you think they are eating. It is an inexact science, and all you can do is your best. I say it that way because you might be certain the bass are hanging around for mackerel when they are really on mullet—and maybe both. Moreover, they might take what you are throwing at them anyway. Note how the bait is behaving for an indication of whether it has been molested by stripers in recent tides. For example, bait herded against a jetty that won't leave may have been trapped and stunned in recent tides. When walking or driving along a beach, if there are unexplained wash-ups of squid, sperling, shad, or sand eels, to name only some, they have to have been ambushed by something. If you spot half a baitfish, it was not a striper attack but likely that of bluefish.

SLICKS

In the daytime it is possible to detect slicks from both stripers and blues. A slick looks like what a drop of oil on water might look like. Sometimes the slick is in one place and the fish are elsewhere, but looking for slicks can pay off. Blues tend to leave large oily slicks, maybe 50 to 100 feet in diameter, and there can be any number of them. Stripers, on the other hand, leave individual slicks the size of a patio table. You may not catch any more than those casters who do not know what to notice, but it is a great icebreaker when meeting other surf fishers.

SMELLING STRIPERS

There are few situations when you will smell stripers. My experience has been that for each time I have ever located bass via smell, there have been fifty phonies who claimed they could smell them even when the wind was wrong—when it was blowing over their shoulders, taking any scent (if there were any) away from them. Still, there can be situations when a definable scent is given off by the digestive activity of bass. What complicates it is that bluefish—and they rarely travel alone—can give off a similar smell.

I don't think it possible to compare the smell of stripers to something with which everyone is familiar. I always think of stripers as smelling less pungent than bluefish and both of them as less obvious than the scent of bunker or menhaden, the latter also never traveling alone. Comparisons to melon or thyme are often used to define the bass smell, but I have not been around melon much. Nevertheless, smelling stripers is not some rare skill reserved for old surfcasters trying to puff their image. If the wind is right, you will know it is fish.

As with slicks, what you identify is digestive processes. For smell to occur in measurable amounts, there must be a large enough number of schooled-up fish that have previously fed off bait at the same time. The condition is also dependent upon intensity, because fresh-air dilution could lower the scent below detection. Any lone striper that ate a sea worm or crab yesterday is not going to be perceptible. When you smell stripers, you are detecting large-scale activity. I suppose you risk misidentifying a school of menhaden as a school of bass, but the distinction might be academic in that if you smell the bait, it could be as meaningful as smelling the bass themselves.

You can be downwind of a school, but how far downwind? Even when winds are right, scent is only rarely a viable means for locating stripers. Moreover, if they have fed enough to stink up the seascape, not only are they less likely to show interest in your fly, but they won't even be in range. I have been into huge schools of bass hundreds of times and never smelled a thing. However, I still view smell as a viable tool in the midwatch hunt for stripers. It only takes once.

Years ago we blitzed fish with regular tackle on the Back Beach in Provincetown but lost track of them when a front came through, changing the wind and pelting us with bouncing rain. Everyone was leaving, lightning laying jagged tracks across the sky, a perfect excuse for looking forward to a warm, dry bunk. I smoked back then, and my pipe filled the buggy with acrid smoke that gagged my poor wife, Joyce. So she rolled down her window enough to breathe. About a mile northwest of where we had blitzed the fish, with her continuing to take in the freshness of the onshore wind, she shouted to me, "Stop!" Here was someone who knew nothing of smelling striped bass, yet what little air drifted in through her small window opening in the gale carried to her the smell of stripers. Stepping out of the buggy on the lee side, I knew right away that it was worth a cast. Joyce, who had difficulty opening her door, sought frantically to get out and join me, and I was immediately on to a moby striper before she could even get— bent horizontal—to the rod racks. In the darkness we could only guess how stacked they were out there, but we could feel the writhing, the misses, the bad takes, and the solid hits that brought the hookups. That memorable blitz, the images of which I will take to my grave, was a gift from my wife's inadvertent sniff.

BREAKING FISH

Anglers learn early to look for collections of working birds because they indicate bait and usually gamefish. After that the issue is whether they are close enough to shore for fishing. Robust bursts of white can be anything—pollack, albacore, bonito, bluefish, or stripers. Further, the sizes of these white puffs do not necessarily indicate which species is out there. All you can do is watch and wait.

Breaking fish at night are another story. You are not going to know they are working unless they are in your fore within casting distance. On beaches with surf, you will often hear them between waves. In estuaries, on the other hand, you will—like fishing in a lake—hear them banging away. Big fish work big and can sound like cinder blocks dropped out of an aircraft, but often it is the kind of bait they are working that inspires a more robust splash. Big bass can also sip softly if they are taking worms or shrimp.

On noisy nights, the surf pounding, perhaps windswept—the elemental fury that Frank Woolner used to talk about—breaking fish, if they are close, will appear as black stains on a gray surf, even on the dark of a new moon. Of course the stains can appear in a quiet bay without you hearing them. All this stuff is a question of intensity, so you mustn't daydream.

STRIPER DIGS

Occasionally you will catch linesides with their chins worn raw and scratchy, clear evidence that they have been rooting on the bottom. I know of three forage species—although there may be others—that will cause them to do this: sea worms, blood worms, and sand eels. Once you have seen stripers probe the bottom for bait in shallow water, their tails and dorsals breaking the surface, struggling to maintain their balance the way you and I might when trying to stand on our heads, it is easy to recognize that they do this. Many places where they dig it is not possible to know they have been doing it unless their chins are abraded. Yet where there is fine sand, as is found on Outer Cape Cod, if you are on the bars at low tide, you will sometimes find little "bunny holes" the size of half a grapefruit on the bottom. You can feel them with your feet. This may not be the most important aspect of locating bass, but I know of no one who has ever reported it, serving to remind us how little is known about our prey. One of the exciting things about surfcasting for striped bass, and fly fishing in particular, is that all the apples have not been picked. As I writer I am always watching for issues, techniques, and discoveries because these observations are what keep my writing alive.

Surfcasters are detectives, so do not discount anything. The discovery of these "digs" is dependent upon perfect conditions that permit both their advent and their preservation. On exposed bars, the holes are filled in by wave action. Because you cannot go over your waders, your search is limited to water deep enough to preserve them, so anything that you find represents only a fraction of the true level of activity. Moreover, it is highly unlikely this action occurred during the day or a Polaroid-equipped surfcaster would be able to see the dusky forms of moving stripers in sunlight. Because digs are still there, they had to have been made last night, and if you are not smart enough to go back tonight, you are reading the wrong book and I am writing it for the wrong person.

STOMACH CONTENTS

Never kill a striper without examining its stomach contents. Sometimes, even when you think you have their number because you have done well fishing, you learn something about striper foraging this way that adds to your store of understanding. Knowing what they have been feeding on is one of those little extras that go with having an occasional fish to eat. Such autopsies often tell more than you expected while yielding surprises about the available forage. As with the masked hatches of fresh water, where you find the fish full of something other than what they were supposed to be feeding upon, you learn to understand the abundance of feeding opportunities available to them. Along with an occasional fishhook, I have seen everything that swims, crawls, digs, or wriggles in the Atlantic as stomach contents.

Known forage like menhaden, alewives, mackerel, sand eels, sperling, pollack, weakfish, snapper blues, mullet, and even juvenile bass are common. Estuarine goodies like grass shrimp, mummichogs, and hatched-out worms can be prevalent. However, your eyes will roll when you find winter flounder neatly stacked like pancakes. You stop worrying about what stripers might eat when they are so loaded with porgies, there is no room for the fly they took. I have found mantis shrimp, which is marine life that I had to identify from scientific journals. Small lobsters are common in a bass belly. Books say that the old Charles Church world-record 73-pounder had a 3-pound lobster in her when caught.

Fly choice begins with what you think they are eating.

MAPPING YOUR WAY

I am always looking for new fishing spots, and I would be a world-class fool if I found them only via driving the thousands of miles of shore that I can reach. By looking for the right kind of geography—and you can only be intimate with geography by seeing it on a map first—it is possible to locate estuaries and prominent points. I have found that the most reliable of maps are published by DeLorme. That company has mapped all of the Striper Coast, state by state, and probably the whole country. I have all of the DeLorme atlases for the Northeast, which I utilize for hunting as well as for fishing. For all locations, with fine-scale maps, you can measure walking and driving distances to determine the feasibility of a spot, the location of a stream, the placement of an outflow, the height of a climb, or the presence or absence of an access road. Sometimes a map can help with something as simple as reading about a great bass caught somewhere and finding where it was supposedly caught on your map. You no doubt have dividers somewhere in your desk, left over from your drawing classes. Set these on the map's scale and you can "walk" the distances on the map page and determine, with great accuracy, just how far you have to go.

The Night Fishing Imperative

For many of us fishing from shore, the notion of doing so at night is not a welcome one. It is unnatural to engage in any activity at a time when our culture teaches that we should be sleeping. Still, like raccoon hunting with a pack of hounds or soaking worms for springtime bullheads, two activities that would never even be thought of during the day, striper fishing from shore, regardless of tackle choice, is a nighttime game. It is hard for me to justify night fishing because I have fished the striper surf at night for so long, so intensely, that it almost did not occur to me that night fishing needed mention. When else would you fish a beach for striped bass? Were it not for my many years of exposure to other surfcasters, it would not even be a viable subject for consideration here. Still, we are not all the same, and I am fully aware of how unwelcome the notion of doing something exclusively at night will be with readers. What would *you* do if you were writing this? Would you sugarcoat and misrepresent fly fishing the striper surf with glamorous sunny photos while preaching the joys and pleasures of a day at the beach? Or would you tell the truth about how it *has* to be done?

There is nothing new or particularly profound about defining fly fishing the striper surf as necessarily a nighttime activity. What may surprise some readers—as much as it distresses me—is that few books intended to teach fishing like this one devote adequate attention to the subject. Indeed, I am bewildered by the paucity of night fishing literature in a culture that so worships both its prose and basic truths. Could it be that striper writers do not know of the importance of night fishing? I doubt it. Might they lack suitable illustration for something they know is important, permitting only a cursory men-

The night fishing imperative is surfcasting's salvation.

tion in some inconsequential way so as to avoid having to take pictures at night? Might they avoid the subject of night fishing as flagrantly as they do because they do not want to be the messenger for information that surely will challenge their readers? When I start telling my readers what they want to hear, I am certain they will stop listening. They should.

You do not have to be a striper fisher to imagine the conspicuous end result of devotion to an activity best done and most rewarding at night. The staggering, narcoleptic surfcaster's entire life is compromised by these maddening and demanding hours. A result is that there is little room in anyone's life after providing for a family along with the acquisition of suitable rest to spend the night fishing for the wily striper. Invariably, if something has to be dropped, it is not likely to be fishing. This pull-in-all-directions situation often, but not necessarily, brings on irreversible consequences either at home or at work; any individual who stays married, advances in his career, and fishes enough to stop staring at the bedroom ceiling ought to get a medal. In addition, you know you are in trouble when you lament having to use sick leave when you are really sick.

There is something counterintuitive about fishing in the dark. It takes a couple of years to get over the idea that what you are pursuing sees what you cannot, in an environment where you cannot function. These anthropomorphic notions about fish and fisherman inspire no small amount of the junk science upon which striper fishing thrives. The next stage is thinking like a fish—clear sign you are over the edge. Thus the fly fishers of the striper surf mumble and stagger over to the vise to tie another fly in winter and to another estuary or beach the rest of the time. Surfcasters, and fly fishers in particular, are really never rid of the compulsion. Even nights when they are not fishing, they toss and moan under the sheets that somebody, somewhere, just might be doing it without them. It is that compelling.

Then there are those who don't make the cut because of darkness. If a lifetime in the striper surf has taught me anything, it is that some people never get over their fear of darkness. Even DEATH BEFORE DISHONOR–tattooed ex-marines were spoiled by too many nights moving around in darkness with an armored infantry division. In the striper surf you go alone. I know, as I have watched them.

They pull up at some hot spot on the beach and they have to shine their light in the surf to check for sea monsters. Before they move on they shine their light over their rod racks to check for snakes; before they get into their buggy, they make certain there are no gorillas in the backseat. Closet boat fishermen, it is only a matter of time before they grapple with a king's ransom in electronics, docking fees, and sunscreen. They are bad for surfcasting's image anyway.

DAY FISHING EXCEPTIONS

There are times when you will catch stripers in the day, but these exceptions are unreliable and distressingly few when measured against the backdrop of night results. One of the most memorable blitzes I ever experienced in daylight happened in August—the worst possible

This successful angler found bass during the night but really cashed in on the magical time of dawn.

month—on Nauset Beach, the best possible place. It was not fly fishing, but I have had three thousand good nights of fishing since.

Autumn, it has long been known, often provides suitably good day
fishing when migrants are on vast schools of baitfish of all species and
sizes. Bass, as well as other marine gamefish, throw all caution to the
wind, wildly corralling whatever is around, competing for what is
there, and wasting little time perusing your offer for fear of losing a
foraging opportunity. Even then, whatever level of blitz occurs during
the day, you will usually see a multiple of it the next night.

I have often started a night at sunset running into a school of
gamefish that has stacked up on a tide rip to feed. I have also seen a
big bass lolling in the first wave and had it take a well-placed cast.

Most of the big bass that I have caught fly fishing were taken in the
day, but always as an extension of a good night. We were just making
the most of daybreak, a time when all wildlife loses its mind for reasons that defy explanation. Ask any deer, turkey, or duck hunter, or
any salmon or trout fisherman. If you quit a night of fishing when
there is a dull glow in the east, do not tell anyone you read my books.
My cardiologist would have to hold a gun to my head before I would
miss the dawn—a magical time.

SALT WATER'S SEQUENTIAL DEVELOPMENT

All my life I have witnessed the sequential development of saltwater
fishermen. They begin by going to the shore in daylight, learning
quickly that night fishing is the secret. After a few years of working
through a progression of numbers, then size, they begin to recognize
that those fishing in boats get ten times the fish and more big fish because they are culling from a greater number. After switching to boat
fishing, which in and of itself leads through a continuum of ever-larger
boats, they learn that boat fishing at night, while dangerous, holds the
greatest promise. Somewhere along the way, they settle upon day fishing in boats because it is more natural to function in daylight. In the
end, though, it is night fishing that got them to where they are.

Casting Distance

Just how far we are able to deliver a fly can be a factor in our successful fishing. Certainly, the more water we reach, the more gamefish we
reach. It would be foolhardy to argue against any measure of compe-

tence in what we do. Having said that, I am tempted to make the case against its importance because, for most of the fishing in which we engage, the bass are often at our feet in the same way the trout and salmon are. Distance is significant, but not as much so as choosing the right pattern in the right place at the right level in the water column. Were I to be assured that an angler would not compromise what is significant in favor of distance, then I might be more willing to endorse distance as a critical factor.

Taking Behavior: How Stripers Attack Flies

How stripers take is governed by what they are feeding upon, the water's action, the amount of bait, and the evident level of competition. I'm convinced that bass behavior is subject to these outside influences. How else can you explain tonight's solid pull, which feels like a fly has simply been seized, as opposed to the experience of the night before when the hit was a violent smash that startled you out of your waders? When linesides are digging for sand eels or sea worms, feeding actions that are similar, old bucket mouth will slurp your fly and stay right there to continue digging. In that case the hit comes as a simple, firm stoppage of the fly.

On the other hand, competing bass that are schooled up tend to be more reckless, slamming your offering before its neighbor, adding fuel to the notion that they know their opportunities are at risk. They don't want to be beaten to the good munchies. It could be, although we do not know, that another influence on taking behavior is what and how much of the area's forage is in their bellies. I know that you and I attack a dish of gravy-laced pasta more quickly after a day in the mines than we would two hours after filet mignon.

Feeding behavior is also influenced by bait's natural ability to function—how well they travel in the sea, how well they escape. I think there are times when bass view late-summer hickory shad booking along at high speed along a beach and say to themselves, *I'm not up for this.* The attitude stems from knowing that shad are agile swimmers; a striper can burn nearly as many calories in pursuit as it can gain from a successful forage. I have seen big bass, back when there were more big bass, slamming shad in the first wave, and it was almost scary—grenades going off. Similarly, I have seen huge summer squid—18 inches long—on Cape Cod being blasted by decent stripers. In the shad example I was unable to determine the combination. With the squid, on the other hand, a popper was the ticket, but it had to be big and fast. Both situations failed to respond to fly fishing—the forage was simply too large.

Occasionally stripers will nudge and reject your fly. Maybe some people know why they do this, but I can no more explain such behavior while fly fishing than I ever could while using either live baits or plugs, which they will nudge as well. They might be full so that less importance is placed upon passing up your offering. They might have been released enough times that they are on to the notion that they are being fished. One night in the summer of 1999 while Joyce and I fished an outflow in Rhody's Narragansett Bay, we both experienced little picks—something was seizing the fly but was never there when we hauled back. There was life, but our concerns mounted that it was *intelligent life*. A couple of times when I ran into this maddening behavior I just marked how much line I had thrown, avoided moving my feet, and sought to replicate the cast that had drawn the pick. Sometimes, after a few picks, or nudges, or pushes, the bugger would come back and take it down. Another night, during a drift when I was fumbling with my fly case, flashlight, and wader straps, hands and mind occupied, I had a rejection tug, and because I was slow reacting the antagonist came back after the little zing and struck in earnest. Sure that I had learned something about striper conduct from this, I told Joyce to *not* pull on the next tug, but just let it swing. Before long I heard her "Jeepers!" "What happened?" I asked. "Forgot and pulled," she answered. She repeated the cast. "Jeepers!" "Try to think of something else. Don't pull!"

"I'm on!"

That morning, on the way home, me critiquing, she nodded and slid against the strain of her seat belt. "We got their number now," I said. No answer. *We got their number now,* I thought. Zzzzzz.

Two weeks later, same tide—"They are doing it again," Joyce said. "Don't pull."

"I didn't," she said.

Some of those bass pulled or nudged the fly as many as four times without actually taking it down. I *think* they were bass, anyway, because we never caught any that night. However, we have taken them when they were acting that way.

Rough water seems to add a measure of abandon to striper behavior. A busy sea can add so much motion to the offering that linesides are forced to move quickly and without a more cautious look at the fly. Nevertheless, rough water also carries its own disadvantages for fly fishers. Impossible winds, seas that act upon your stripping, and vicious landing problems when big fish—say, over 20 pounds— are lying in the surf sliding back and forth in water too mean for you to go down and make a move all provide their own challenges. Regardless of your tackle choice, it is part of surfcasting to know when to change, move, or pack it in.

Big Stripers

Some surf fishers pride themselves in taking big stripers. This predilection toward monsters springs from knowing that a majority of people—whether bait fishing, plugging, or even fishing from boats— are out fishing for anything they can get. Most anglers are happy to find stripers, or any other species for that matter, and any level of success, even with small fish, is fine with them. In contrast, the sharpies make a directed effort toward trophy stripers. When anglers have had enough schoolies, they begin to recognize that the only remaining stone in the road is size. Consequently, they become more conscious of how they expend their energies, learning quickly that great numbers of school bass become repetitious—you can spend the night fighting fish that have come out of the same mold.

SMALL FISH DISTRACT

There are also some serious conservation issues involved with spending the night releasing one small striper after another when it is known that even in release fishing there is a mortality rate. Every once in a while you will see a pink stain running down a striper's flank from a gill injury. You can put it out of your mind, but that released bass is stuck with the injury. I cringe when someone brags about having caught "several hundred" bass in a season then complains about how many fish are killed commercially.

In spring there are places that have been known for half a century to consistently produce the first stripers. All of them, every one that I can name, provide zero opportunity for even a 20-inch fish. Lines of anglers are on all through the tide, catching and releasing, because a striper of any size is viewed as a celebration of the seasons. Moreover, these small fish get people started in spring a full month before arrival of the sexually mature fish that we dream about. Ultimately, these same surfcasters are so exhausted from having chased around the Striper Coast for six months—and their wives are tired of having slept alone as well—that a full six weeks before the last striper has left the territory, they cannot stand another sleepless night. Furthermore, it is the big bass that are passing in migration from as far away as the Maritimes in November and December, when the air is 30 and the water is 60, snow dancing over a steaming sea.

Most marine species school according to size. If they did not, larger bass would forage on smaller ones. Humans gasp at this "cannibalism," but in the world of fish that is the way it is. That is why it is possible, depending upon spawning success fifteen and twenty years before, for any of us to find ourselves among a school of linesides that are all over 40 inches. Conversely, if you have not seen it already, you will some night find yourself among enough stripers the size of perch to feel their writhing on your line, the water shimmering from their many movements like fat sizzling. Fish on every cast.

It is incumbent upon trophy hunters, therefore, to make clear choices and move from the small fish and keep looking for the better ones. There is a range of sizes in striper schools, where 3-pounders are often found with a sprinkling of 10-pounders. We have all kept fishing, fighting and releasing the little ones, in the hope of that occasional 10. Sometimes you have to cull your way through the many schoolies for that one night-saving fish, that keeper.

SMALL FISH TEACH

The process of learning what stripers like in a given situation never ends. Having caught my first bass over fifty years ago—on a sea worm drifted from a bridge on the Warren River in Rhode Island at age fourteen—I have never stopped learning about striper behavior. A common goal to which we should all dedicate ourselves is the search for the perfect fly. No matter how often we do well, there is always another material that can be applied to our list of fly dressings—known loosely as a fly pattern—to move a lineside more quickly than yesterday's killer. Also, fly tying has never been more exciting than it is today. For instance, I had never heard of velvet tubing five years before writing this. Yet no less than five distinct patterns that use velvet tubing have emerged from the vises of striper fishermen.

Anytime I have a new idea in a fly, I hold it for one of those nights when the fishing is so good that it is boring. Then I get to experiment with my creations to find out what bass are really fond of—and they do tell. The best part is the surprises.

DOES FLY SIZE CULL?

Plug and live-bait fishermen have long used bigger offerings to cull the larger stripers from a school. It is not perfectly reliable, because we commonly catch 20-inch bass on 10-inch plugs, but it is something that can be done to relieve the frustration of having lesser bass hit ahead of the real monsters. I would try this in fly fishing but advise that the effort might be even more frustrating because fly size cannot be increased as dramatically as plug size. Moreover, while bigger lures reward the angler in most cases with easier casting, bigger flies heap but one more encumbrance on the fly fisher.

FIGHTING BIG STRIPERS

The intimidation a fly fisher experiences when hooking up to big stripers is memorable. Every fly fisher with whom I have ever discussed this agrees that a bass feels much bigger when taken fly fishing; part of this perception springs from having the hit come to the hand rather than the rod. Fly-fishing gear is not necessarily weaker, but spinning and conventional lines—what we must use for any comparison—are evolving and becoming stronger, whereas fly lines remain at the same strength. No matter how much we beef up backing and tippet, the fly-line strength is 30 pounds, and we must retain protection for the fly line by offering a weaker tippet than 30 pounds. Still, world records have been caught with tackle that tested at less than 30, so such fears are not justified. However, big-game behavior is different on fly tackle, and those differences should be addressed.

By design, maximum tippet is 20 pounds. In contrast—unlike, say, 20-pound spinning line—the section of 20-pound tippet in fly fishing is a scant 3 feet at most, defeating all hope of experiencing any stretch. Don't kid yourself: Stretch affords a great deal of protection from the stress of a running lineside. The flex of the rod provides little protection from a break-off because in most cases the rod will be bent to the point where it really can bend no farther. If the rod is that far over, your drag should be giving line to a running fish. How much force

If the rod is this far over, your drag should be giving line to a running fish.

your drag should be accepting before giving line is a judgment call for the angler. The decision is sobering in the face of the fact that increasing amounts of torque as the spool depletes will require almost constant adjustment. The safe thing is to fight all fish with a lighter drag to start and let spool depletion, which is more dramatic in fly fishing, effect its own tightening. You must watch the consumption of backing because the situation is curtains if you run out. The more backing you can keep on that reel, the better chance you have of defeating what will often be a moby striper.

Let's talk more about spool depletion. Because of the thickness of fly lines, the greatest change in mechanical advantage for turning the spool against the drag will occur during the running out of the fly line. You will notice that once you are in the backing, if drag settings are adequate, little adjustment should be necessary. For that reason, a reel giving fly line freely should be considerably tighter once the fly line is out. Backing depletion should be so slow that only an occasional drag adjustment is necessary deep into the reel. What regulars who are experienced in fighting big bass often do is "palm" the spool's rim— what they call rim control—during hard and strong runs. Keep in mind that a single-action fly reel, unlike your counterpart with casting gear, turns only once for each painful crank. I say *painful* because all those wild turns of the reel generated by a good striper have to be brought back with your hand; on average, you will thus crank three and a half times more turns than with a spinning reel.

When you have a bigger bass on, you will occasionally feel blows to your line as though someone were hitting your line with a stick. When you experience this, it is a clear sign the fish has its head and the line is lying across the fish's body, its tail striking the line with each pump as it tries to swim off. You will not gain on this lineside until you turn it in your direction, having the line running from its mouth rather than along the body. And this effort to turn the fish could break your tippet, so you must be cautious.

The good thing about your equipment choices as a fly fisher is that the fly line, with its commensurate thickness, travels poorly through the water and acts like a sea anchor. I have found that once a bass changes direction—which they all do in an effort to try different ways to escape —pulling that fly line full-length through the water kills them.

Joyce palms the spool on a good striper, then follows it down the beach.

Once a trophy striper has been defeated, it gives up readily. Every animal on our planet, including us antagonists, has its limits. Your experience with a particular fish will reveal the moment that its ability to resist begins waning. When such defeat is evident, the balance of effort versus gain will tip into your favor and you will see that the return of backing has the game going for your team.

There is no shame in chasing a fish down the beach, either to prevent the loss of backing or to more easily gain backing for the reel. Your boat-fishing counterpart gets to back down with the help of a motor, often having the assistance of another person to control that motor. You, on the other hand, get to chase your monster down the beach only on those rare occasions when it happens to go the right way. You will really appreciate what I mean when your cranking hand goes dead. But, ah, the old bugaboo of wondering what you did wrong when a fish is dropped has no more meaningful answer with the fly than it does with meat on the bottom. An unknown quantity of steel penetrates an unknown quantity of fish flesh, and hooks pull free. It happens to all of us, and the shrink's waiting room is full of people who have had the experience.

Monsters in the Wind

Some places are famous for harboring the best stripers on the planet. Places like Cuttyhunk, Rhode Island, Montauk, Cape Cod, and Plum Island, to name only some, all take their turn playing host to fish-of-the-year. Still, a thousand unnamed hot spots in between are visited by a school of dream bass undetected while ten mysteriously give up a few memorable linesides. The shore-fishing detective who finds out that it is happening somewhere, assuming he is not distracted by a bunch of schoolies, gets something to work on in the moving water he can find in the deep of night.

Anytime that you locate good fishing, there is a strong chance of a repeat in striper behavior on the next night tide. The best fishing I have ever experienced was nearly always the product of following up on previous blitzes. Bass simply come back. Certainly, the reasons for them to be in a given location are likely to occur again the next time conditions are similar. Of those environmental factors reliable enough to include here, the night and tide are sufficiently predictable. Anything else that you suspect of having inspired the fishing should also be considered. The presence of bait, wind direction, boat traffic, a rising sun—all play into the observable mix that can either influence fish behavior or play no part at all. It's a strange game with primitive rules.

Fishing Reports: A Grain of Salt

When outdoor magazines conduct reader surveys, they invariably indicate that fishing reports are the most popular feature; subscribers go to them first. Nonetheless, many readers have told me that they have had firsthand experience fishing somewhere when it was bad, and later read of a blitz where they had been. A common complaint is when a northeast storm comes through, turning the shore upside down; the next week's fishing reports say it was good, and there is no mention of the impossible conditions that any memory would recall. I cite these examples to emphasize how reports can be suspect.

Why is this? I never did reports, but I think it is a little of everything. Perhaps some shops paint glowing reports to encourage anglers to come down to buy bait and tackle. I also think that occasionally the contributor may be suspicious of some reports but feels that as long as he can quote the interview, he is off the hook. For example, "Joe's B&T says that the Jersey shore is blitzing in moby stripers." If it is not true, we can blame Joe and not the reporter. Some reporters have told me that they don't pass on obvious exaggerations. In addition, there is the tackle shop problem of always seeing people going fishing and never seeing them coming back—they only stop at tackle shops on their way out. Some anglers want to be big vaqueros when they catch a nice fish and strut over it, but they still want to lie about where they caught it, so they say they got it in your spot to keep heat off their own.

The impossible time element changes things, and readers are expected to know that. I have seen many instances where the situation was being reported upon accurately. For example, we were blitzing fish last September in Rhode Island, and it was accurately reported the next week. Sure, some reports are off the mark, but a majority of them are not bad. Taking them with a grain of salt, I read them all.

Conversely, the Internet commonly carries information that is posted anonymously by some irresponsible, immature "children" who are simply vandalizing a Web site or purposely deceiving other anglers. Anonymity renders just about everything posted on the Internet highly suspect, and I would never make or alter fishing plans by what is written there.

The Angling Mind

While luck plays a part in every game, it can take any of us only so far. The better angler recognizes the reduced role of luck while appreciating a heightened contribution from the angling intellect. In the long run, the most significant component any individual can possess remains the mind that flourishes when spiced with knowledge. Consistent success comes back like the lyrics of a familiar song. Those with experience bask in the confidence of playing with house money.

If over fifty years of hunting and fishing have taught me anything, it is that few people ever learn what it takes to succeed in the outdoors. They are always in search of that one element they believe holds the keys to the castle. The guy in New Jersey thinks he is fishing in the wrong state. His Connecticut counterpart believes there is a magical fly pattern that will catch all the stripers all the time. In Maine the big fish are south. In Massachusetts they are north. Long Island is too crowded and the Montauk fishermen long and pine for a less fettered world. Hog-tying themselves to eternal pessimism, they work harder at finding excuses for their bad fishing rather than seeking the solutions.

Skillful fly fishing in the striper surf is not a longer cast, a perfect fly height in the water column, designer clothes, or signature tackle at some yet-to-be-discovered stage of tide. Instead, it is an understanding of the mix of method, environment, conditions, prey, and how these things influence one another.

Keep the fish in the water with a minimum of handling.

Having known hundreds of surfcasters, with woefully few dedicated to the fly, those who caught fish when there really were very few never possessed some singular insight into the striper surf. On the contrary, their boundless optimism was fueled by the confidence in what they did and the joy of doing it.

Fishing Factors in Order of Importance

1. Night fishing

2. The angling mind

3. Conditions

4. Breaking fish

5. Bait

6. Monsters in the wind

7. Focusing on large fish

8. Casting distance

2 Equipment

Equipment choices are an exciting part of fly fishing. Certainly, the true fun of any outdoor activity is putting the tools in our hands that will enable us to both fish with comfort and catch our quarry with impunity. Still, in the final analysis, the performance difference between a hundred-dollar rod and a handcrafted split-bamboo wand costing many thousands probably cannot be measured, and the value of the latter is more likely a state of mind than a significant advantage in fly fishing.

There is a serious trend in evidence among all fishing interests toward viewing equipment as the key to great fishing. People believe that with the right equipment they will enjoy more success, as measured in both quantity and size of striped bass. I have been made acutely aware of this trend through my online associations with hundreds of surfcasters on a message board I have administered for four years. In effect, average fishermen are way more concerned with equipment issues, as they apply to the striper surf, than with the natural history of their adversary, the understanding of the lineside's environment, and the behavioral idiosyncrasies of the species. Indeed, thinking is so skewed that most surfcasters would place equipment way above conditions in any ranking of surfcasting issues by importance when, in my

opinion, it is the understanding of conditions that holds the true secrets of the striper old-timers. And while it would thrill me to put a stop
to these trends, I am also acutely aware they are not likely to change.

Some fly-fishing product developments are so effective that they
produce a profound change in how we fish and rig for fishing. Others
promise to revolutionize our sport, but fit nicely with the needs of
only some. Still others would be better left decaying in warehouses. A
related complexity is that few authors are likely to know all that is
available. Developments after publication further exacerbate the risk
of antiquated choices. We writers would thus prefer to discuss the
conditions and behavioral traits that stripers exhibit, because they do
not change. The relationship between nature and man's response to

**Good equipment makes fly fishing easier and more
pleasurable.**

those developments is what must be understood. The problems themselves never change—only the means that we employ to deal with them. Something to keep in mind throughout this discussion on equipment.

In my fifty-five years of fly fishing, I have witnessed a marvelous evolution in the development of equipment that is likely to continue long after my passing. If history is any teacher, our rods will become lighter, stronger, and more effective. Similarly, our reels will carry more backing, weigh less, cost less, and snub down the biggest stripers in our surf with smooth drags protecting unbreakable lines. In contrast, my first trout caught while fly fishing was mastered with pure junk, and my first striper on a fly twenty years later was taken with tackle that no one would fish with today. In fact, what I use to fly fish the striper surf now is both a testimony to progress and a pleasure to use. Further, I would not dare think that evolution is over. Thus I am reluctant to devote any earnest discussion to the subject of equipage. To do so would doom and date this book through a succession of obsolescence. Yet there are certain constants that have not altered in my time, which suggests that they will not in the future.

Fly Rods

If you are in pursuit of a quarry that could exceed 50 pounds, and placed in a situation where using any kind of watercraft would not be an option, you can never have too heavy a rod. The determinant then for just how large a rod you should use is your own strength. Two functions come into play in rod choice: delivery of the line through casting, and fighting the fish. If you consider the pool-cue rods used in spinning and conventional surfcasting, no fly rod is likely to be too stiff for taming stripers. And the heaviest line you can use will be more functional in the windy settings found on the Striper Coast. Rods ranging from 8 to 12 weight are suitable for most people. For men of average strength and build, a 10- or 11-weight rod is appropriate. For most women, assuming they are not from the World Wrestling Federation, an 8- or 9-weight rod is suitable. Individual preference in rod length is always important, but I find the bulk of saltwater fly rods offered by the big-name companies in the industry are 9 feet, and that is a length I have come to like.

There is a recognizable trend toward stiffer rods for their rating than was the norm only a few years ago. For example, a 10-weight rod flexed more back then. Try attaching a weight to two horizontal rods—an older one and a new one—and measuring the deflection. These days you will find stiffer rods for a given rating than were offered before. I think, though I really do not know, that rod makers would prefer casters not overload their rods so that they are not broken while casting. Thus, less flexible rods do not cast as well unless they are forced to flex with a heavier line.

My first striper fly rod was fiberglass and it was used to tame all my best bass. Today Joyce and I fish with graphite, and the materials are changing. In this application, I would also be certain that all rods have a short fighting butt, which is usually offered anyway on rods rated over 8. The fighting butt is necessary to keep the wildly spinning reel of a run away from your chest, and to keep your hand clear while reeling in line.

There has been a recent trend toward two-handed Spey rods that are up to 14 feet long for use on big fish like tarpon, salmon, and stripers. I can make no statement about the functionality of such equipment in the striper surf. However, I do know that those who use them speak highly of them and find advantages in weight distribution of the rod, greater casting distances, and a certain novelty in their use. Of course, if the rod makers had their way we would all have a special rod for bluefish, a perfect one for Tuesdays, and another for bluefish on Tuesdays, and do it all over again for striped bass the other six nights (the way I do with books). I think that if you do everything else right fly fishing for stripers, and you like the way Spey rods deliver line, then using one might be a good idea.

Fly Lines

The easiest fly line to use is a floater, and the most practical choice is a weight forward. You will find that in 90 percent of the situations with which you are confronted, a floating line is your best choice. Still, because of the aforementioned manufacturer tendency toward underrating rods, I always use a line one rating higher than recommended. My 10-weight rod is fished with an 11 line. The casting advantages are obvious, and neither my wife nor I has ever broken a fly rod while fishing.

There has been a growing trend toward the use of intermediate-sink-rate fly lines. Most manufacturers champion their use both to sell more lines—like the Tuesday fly rods—and to advance the notion that the intermediate line is a more direct connection to the fly and gamefish. While this makes sense, the reduction of slack between angler and gamefish is really inconsequential when measured against the violence in the take of saltwater species. I fish with an intermediate roughly half the time and see no difference in performance.

The array of situations with which you will be confronted in the striper surf calls for lines of varying sink rates. You will often find it necessary to fish deep runs where the fly has to get down fast or it will be swept away first. When stripers are digging for worms or sand eels, that floating line we all love so much is way over their heads, where they cannot even see it. All fishing is applied efficiency, and waiting all night for your line to sink is a waste of precious fishing time. A sinking fly line enables you to present a fly at the level at which stripers are feeding. Some inlets, the ones that can sweep you to Portugal before you can find your cell phone, call for a Deep-Water Express or lead-core. Get the fly to their kitchen in any way you can. Because we are fishing the beach here, it is not as important to have a wide array of sink rates in our fly lines as it is for those who are fishing from boats. Most of your water-column demands will be minimal because of an almost constant exposure to shallows.

Never leave home with only one line. If there is anything that is likely to go wrong, it is the line. Also, changing spools to get you back into the action—should a line get broken off at the backing, tangled in the stones of some barnacle-encrusted jetty, or hopelessly gnarled at your feet or in your basket—is one more way to rescue the night. Be cautious about the use of insect repellents when fly fishing. Those that contain DEET can ruin the coating on a fly line.

Shooting heads, which are lower in cost and only 30 or 40 feet long, cast differently in that they are faster in the backcast and harder to use into a wind. The head is heavier than the running line and pulls the running line out through the guides easily. This enables you to heave the line awesome distances with little or no false casting. Offered in a variety of sink rates, these heads can be quickly changed with loop-to-loop connections.

For many years Scientific Anglers has offered the Concept fly line for beginners and occasional anglers; it has a shorter taper and head that really speed up the learning process for people new to fly fishing. They also have a Headstart in their Mastery Series intended to meet the same needs. Teaching our children how to fly fish, we have found these lines invaluable tools.

Fly Reels

If there is a bad guy in equipment, it is the reel. Fly casting is the only type of saltwater casting that is done with one arm. Because of this, even weight lifters get a tired casting arm, and where women are concerned—as with my wife and daughters—the reel is the albatross. The reason for this is that the reel has to hold a large, thick fly line plus 200 yards of backing, *and* be equipped with a drag suitable for rhinos. Those nice itty-bitty, less-than-4-ounce fly rods are not much use when the reel weighs a pound. In other words, dear and patient reader, the fly reel is what sends surfcasters home early. When shopping for a suitable fly reel, look for the least number of trade-offs in weight, backing capacity, and drag efficiency. Once you are sure you like the reel, then buy extra spools for it. An array of turned 6061 bar-stock aircraft aluminum fly reels have lately stormed the market and taken much of the curse out of the reel's role in the equipment quandary. Truly, finely crafted anodized aluminum borders on jewelry.

What I have done in selecting a reel for my wife, Joyce, is select something with a rugged drag that is meant for a smaller-line-weight outfit. Then I upped the backing capacity on this smaller reel by cutting off the bottom 20 feet of fly line, which she never casts to anyway. Backing in this case is 30- or 40-pound braid, enabling us to hold even more toward the comfortable 200 yards. Promise not to laugh, but the older I get, the more I use her outfit when she is nodding in the buggy. (The older she gets, the more often she nods.)

There is a nagging and persistent controversy regarding which hand should be used for cranking a fly reel. Proponents of the left hand say that doing so allays the need to move the rod from one hand to the other after the fight starts. Old-guard conventional surfcasters like myself are more familiar with holding the rod with the left and reeling with the right. It is a debate with neither a solution nor useful consequence.

Backing

Many of the new superlines provide us with strength without diameter, which, on paper, means we can carry more backing with less reel. However, if the reel is too small, it lacks a big-game drag. What we should all be worrying about with these superlines is their abrasive nature because some of them, if not all, will saw through the snake guides of that nice Thomas & Thomas you paid a ransom for in only a couple of nights of fishing. Never forget that a night of striper fishing—assuming you have read all my books—commonly has you beaching fifteen or more stripers, with twelve having gone into your backing. That is a lot of abrasion to pack into a few nights of fishing. Grooved guides eat fly lines.

Backing should always be way stronger than the weakest connection in your setup because it is changed the least often. I use 50-pound Dacron braid. It is large enough for easy handling during an encounter with a moby striper, and does not exhibit outrageous abrasion.

Leaders

No manufacturer that I have found offers a suitably tapered big-game leader. If the tippet end is strong enough, the large end drops too fast in diameter when compared to the thickness of the fly line. The obvious solution is to taper your own by knotting different sizes of leader material. Besides, trimming the tippet end with normal fly changes, you lose track of the true strength of the tippet on factory-tapered leaders.

Keep in mind that in those special situations where you are using fast-sinking lines, harmony in sink rate between leader and fly line has to be preserved. Otherwise your fly line is dredging the bottom below a slow-sinking leader and fly. Consequently, short leaders that retain a degree of taper are best put together by hand.

You can never be too careful, but I have found that stripers are not overly leader shy. If anything, they are more sensitive to the pattern offered to them, along with its presentation at a level that appeals to them. I find that leader length on floating or on intermediate lines is best at around the rod length—say, 9 feet. I divide up that length with sections of 50, 40, 30, and 20 pounds, leaving that last section a little longer to provide for the changing of flies.

The strength of the above outfit—50-pound backing, 30-pound fly line (and the tests I have performed indicate most fly lines are 30 pound), with leader tippet down to 20 pound—is about as strong as can be assembled. This is important for anyone serious about fly fishing for stripers that commonly reach big-game proportions. We are not livelining fruit flies here. There is no excuse for breaking off in spite of how common such occurrences might be, and if my daughter came home with somebody who broke off regularly I would strain to be polite. (If I didn't shoot the sonovabitch first.)

Waders

The wading needs of fly fishermen are no different from those of other surf fishermen, but a few points should be made. Stockingfoot waders are lighter, more comfortable, and distinctly more suitable for fishing jetties and estuaries. On sandy beaches, where wave action is continuous, sand will invariably work its way into the space between wading shoe and wader. Another disadvantage with stockingfoots is that they are more difficult to put on, giving you the sense of suiting up twice.

What a boat I could have bought with the money spent on waders over the years. Waders are constantly evolving, and I have had them all. The new breathables have promise because they remain waterproof while perspiration vapor escapes. Presently I fish with two styles to accommodate the diverse water temperatures found on the cold Outer Cape and the warm Rhode Island shore—a difference of close to 20 degrees: fly weights for 70-degree water and neoprene for 55.

Always wear a wading belt, because it performs the functions of providing a pocket, creating a waistline, and distributing the weight of the waders. The notion that such a belt will prevent your waders from filling is given way too much attention—water pressure prevents that anyway. Most shore fishermen believe that water entering over the top edge of the waders dooms the fisher to 62 pounds per cubic foot of added weight, which will sink him like a stone. Some even believe that air trapped in the waders will float them helplessly on their heads. Truth is that no such horrors await a person wading either with or without a belt. Extensive testing that I performed while retained by an insurance company involved in litigation over the death of a surf fisherman wearing waders showed that the belt was not a factor. In these tests I splashed about in deep water without a wader belt, trying to run water into the waders. But water pressure on the outside forced the opening against my body, creating a seal that prevented most of the water from coming in while trapping air inside. What little water I did carry was more than compensated for by all the excess air, and I floated around like a child with a rubber toy. Even when I deliberately filled the waders, the added weight was neutralized as long as I stayed in the water; it was only a problem when trying to exit, and you could easily shed that weight once you stood by permitting gravity to pull the waders down. Trapped air in your legs and feet does not float you upside down; if anything—and it will be there either way—it would contribute dramatically to saving your life.

People killed surfcasting, probably two per year on the entire Striper Coast, are most likely victims of other injuries, such as head trauma or panic, that prevent them from allowing the waders to work for them. There are also times when excitement while fishing could bring on a cardiac event, but the surfcaster's survivors will surmise that waders pulled the person down. We'll really never know.

Stripping Baskets

If you interviewed a hundred experienced saltwater fly fishermen to ask about stripping baskets, more than ninety-nine would say that they would not fish without one. Beyond the acceptability of them, healthy debate rages on about whether they should be with or without drain holes, bought from the big fly companies, or made at home with a Rubbermaid pan. Add in the contrivances devised to take them off quickly, and the cone arrangements intended to create fewer tangles, and you have a mix of options in stripping baskets. Some regulars even have two—with and without drain holes to better address the most controversial aspect of their use.

There are many situations fishing the shore that affect the question of basket use. For instance, when using floating lines, a basket is not necessary because the line is going to lie on the surface, *less* likely to tangle in the water than in a basket. The greatest justification for using a basket is sinking lines, but if you grease or dress the running line of a fast-sinking head, you can still forgo the cumbersome basket. I think the need to cast greater distances is what inspires their use more than anything—a factor that gets a lot of attention even in lure casting with spinning and conventional gear. The distance discussion rages in all forms of surf fishing. My answer is always—regardless of angling choice—that it depends upon where you are fishing, how close you are to the fish, and the kind of shore upon which you are

Stripping baskets are popular in the striper surf and are needed in many cases.

standing. Surf is a curse, but curiously, I do much less fly fishing in bank-sliding water where a basket is necessary.

I spent many years enjoying salmon fishing in the Maritimes and never saw a stripping basket in use on big rivers where distance casting is mandatory—but then salmon fishing is all done on the surface. I find that placing stripped line into the basket is a distraction from the fishing and a nuisance when fishing out of a buggy, where moving to a new location along the beach is necessary many times in a night of fishing. Admittedly, my sentiments on the subject could easily come under scrutiny, and nowhere in this book do I sense greater concerns for an opinion that flies into the face of acceptance. I have seen very little use of stripping baskets in fresh water and yet much use in salt. They are popular, though I believe overused.

Don't worry about your waders filling with water. Think about what a container around your waist will do to influence the buoyancy to which you are accustomed. If you are forced to make a deep crossing, an empty stripping basket without holes will float you away in whatever current you are confronted with. If there are holes in the basket, you won't float away; rather, you will have to try to move about while your weight increases to 60 pounds around your waist. With drain holes, a wave will add to your standing weight until the water has drained off. Without drain holes, you will likely fall forward from the sudden increase in weight.

Gaffs

In spite of a growing sentiment to the contrary, a small hand gaff is a necessary part of the surfcaster's equipment because there are bound to be times when you will choose to keep a fish, even if that happens only once or twice in a year. When the time comes to subdue a large striper, the gaff is often—but not always—needed. What a gaff does is put a handle on something that would otherwise be thrashing and splashing about, lunging in all directions. In a moderate surf, a spent bass can be pressured just as a wave is breaking so that it is caught by that wave then washed up onto the wet sand. Yet in an estuary, river, or flat where fishers might be far from shore, those wanting to keep fish would be at an unnecessary disadvantage. Remember that the larger the fish—and those are the ones we are more likely to want to keep—the greater the justification for using a gaff. I can't picture my-self exiting a foaming tidal river with a rod in one hand and my re-maining arm wrapped around a live 50-pounder, a dream fish.

The right tool does not have to be over a foot long, but it does have to be sharp with its tip covered by a section of rubber tubing to pre-vent injury to the carrier. What I have always done is tape the tubing onto the handle so its preload causes it to snap out of the way when slid from the point.

There are also certain jetty situations where a 5- or 6-foot-han-dled gaff is necessary because of your height above the water; still, that is less likely to occur when fly fishing.

I am aware that there is resistance to the use of gaffs in sportfish-ing. A number of Striper Coast states have banned their use, appar-ently from the notion that certain tools kill fish when the truth is that people kill fish. It would be a person short of nuts, bolts, and compe-tent wiring who would gaff a fish he did not intend to utilize. Point is, once a decision is made to reduce a fish to possession, the use of a gaff is of no consequence. Opposition to gaff use has to come from those who have never been confronted with a good striper in a bad place.

The Small Stuff

For many surfcasters a wading staff is a good idea because it serves as a third leg in a potentially dangerous environment where you can eas-ily trip on a stone or slip on the moss of that stone. Ski poles do a nice job of acting as a wading staff after you remove their basket—which takes only a minute. Selectively, depending upon where we are fish-ing, my wife and I both use them.

Regardless of how you cast, a backpack is necessary for walking the shore with a surf rod. Spools, flies, food, water, a thermos, camera, cell phone, insect repellent, a section of rope, a sweater, and a foul-weather top are items that add up to more than any tackle bag is likely to handle. And you have to keep one hand free going in so that you can carry out that monster you are sure to catch after reading this book.

A compass should be a part of every surfcaster's gear. In a lifetime of shore fishing, I have been lost on flats in fog a number of times. I have also made a bad turn on dune roads in fog and driven around in circles an important part of the night. There are places where it is possible to walk or to wade long distances at night in the fog, and you had better find your direction before the tide changes.

If you have a stream thermometer from freshwater fishing, or if you are a person who wants to have everything, knowing the water temperature is useful for determining the beginning and end of striper-fishing seasons. I also believe that you can isolate reasons why fish act a certain way by knowing where the water temperature changes and perhaps why.

Releasing fish does more harm to the angler than the fish. I have found that gripping the lower jaw of a striper exposes my left hand to many small abrasions and some deeply penetrating gill cuts that often get infected. The better the fishing, the nearer my hand comes to hamburger. Years ago our BS meter was set to look at the hands of those who bragged about good fishing because it was a great way to tell. But these days the use of a glove on the gripping hand affords me both protection and easier (consequently safer for the bass) release.

Protect your eyes from bright sun during the day to prevent night blindness. In spite of spending most of your fishing time in darkness,

Use of a glove on the gripping hand affords both angler protection and safety for the bass.

Not just "sunglasses" but Polaroids are what is needed to penetrate surface glare.

there are going to be times—evenings coming on, dawns going off— when penetration of surface glare is necessary, and only polarizing lenses can provide that in sunglasses. With these it is possible to read structure, find baitfish, and even see gamefish cruising along the shore. They are a must.

Flies—The Big Stuff

You will commonly be confronted with schools of undersized bass or even boring numbers of "keepers," which few anglers these days really keep. Barbless hooks enable you to easily release a fish, with less harm likely to either bass or angler. Moreover, penetration of barbless hooks is more efficient than that of hooks with a barb. Some anglers, as a matter of policy, always use them. However, if you are ever involved with a potential trophy-fishing situation where you have the chance at a dream striper—and it happens all the time—you will desperately wish that you had a barb on the hook. Never forget that if barbless hooks are popular because they are easier to remove, they will also *drop* more bass, including perhaps the one for which you have been waiting all your life. It is still your choice.

No fly fisherman could ever worship at the altar of the striper surf without spending considerable time and resources in concern for the flies. We have all stood there—be it in a trout stream, salmon river, or salt flat—wondering what was wrong with our fishing. Undeniably, there will always be times when having the right fly—and all fly fishing is like this—is paramount. However, having dealt with the problem elsewhere, nowhere is it less of an issue than in the striper surf. One reason is that the very nature of your fishing—at night from the shore—means that any stripers around are likely feeding. You will of course be confronted with some selective feeding, and I will talk more about this elsewhere, but most of the time, if you have found stripers, that streamer on your tippet is enough to catch them. Here are some reflections on my favorite striper flies.

SAND EEL FLY (FRANK'S OLD RELIABLE)

When I first discovered fly fishing as a viable choice in surfcasting, I was putting four to seven white saddle hackles on a 3/0 Mustad 34007 hook to catch linesides. Later, and I know it was a head thing, I attached black saddles on the top and gray on the sides in order to create a gradient in color that simulated the millions of sand eels in our surf. I felt that saddle feathers were better than bucktail because the feathers were longer and also more supple. Further, the feathers create a better width-to-length ratio for sand eel imitation. Though primitive by today's fly-tying standards, I fished this pattern for many years without ever wondering if there was something better.

DECEIVERS

This old stock pattern is offered in countless variations that all work. This generic minnow streamer is the fly to use if you know nothing about what stripers are feeding on. My guess is that most anglers rely upon these the most. Having a variety of styles and hook sizes is useful.

GENE QUIGLEY'S BABY ANGEL

This deer hair peanut bunker pattern, along with personal variations, is a must on nights and places where stripers have been feeding on juvenile bunker. On a trip to Maine to visit and fish with our daughter Susan, we found medium stripers in the daytime stacked in a tide rip in Harpswell Sound that would not take any other pattern. We have also used it in Narragansett Bay with marvelous results.

HERRING AND BUNKER VARIATIONS

Bill Catherwood of Boston's North Shore, who is one of the most masterful saltwater tiers I know, once gave me a herring fly that is too nice to fish with. I would cry if a bluefish ever took it away. Still, I think Catherwood personifies both the trend in fly-design sophistication and the advancing levels of success that are taking place in fly fishing. But there is a danger.

The heavier a fly gets, the more difficult it is to fish with when you take into account the added weight in water that the fly absorbs. At some time point, despite the need to simulate both herring in spring and bunker in summer, flies can be too big for effective casting. Peanut bunker, under 3 inches, are never a problem. Also keep in mind that juvenile alewives drop down from natal rivers from late October to mid-November and can be fooled with the same Baby Angel genre of pattern.

Catherwood's Bunker Fly (top) is a peach, but watch fly size and weight, as with this popular red-gill (bottom).

POPPER VARIATIONS

It is always fun to fish with poppers. Seeing a bass come up to smack a popper is a recognized high point in fishing the striper surf. Remember to watch your popper closely because bass commonly follow them without taking. I cannot count the times I have seen bass swirl behind one repeatedly. People who say "He missed it" do not know striped bass. When you are stabbing venison on your plate, do you miss? I learned a long time ago that the bass do not *miss*. If they want your fly, you will have difficulty taking it away from them. I have often bent a streamer on quickly and taken that "swirler" that didn't like the popper.

The reason why I am not wild about popper fishing is that even plug fishing I have never seen anyone get anything that was really that great a catch with one. With other plugs I have taken hundreds of bass over 40 pounds, but I have never caught a 40-pounder on a popper. Don't get me wrong; they are great for bluefish and certain schoolie situations, and I like the same kind of fun things as the next guy. Nevertheless, I have a made a business of documenting experiences in fishing and I just tell it the way I have seen it, despite some of those things being unpopular.

SLIDER VARIATIONS

These are nothing but cork cylinders with a small tuft of deer hair offered in a variety of colors. What you must remember is that, in spite of looking like poppers, they are not poppers and should be fished differently. Sliders should be used in current, cast across the flow, and allowed to swing under tension, creating a subtle wake. Don't pop a slider.

GRASS SHRIMP VARIATIONS

These are must-have flies in certain estuarine situations where you either see the shrimp or find them in striper stomachs. I have had great fishing when the stripers were displaying selectivity because they were feeding on shrimp—a common consequence. If shrimp are the suspected forage, you can usually draw shrimp to you by turning on your light a foot in front of your waders. They will be drawn to the light. There are some nice molded rubber shrimp around in tackle shops. If you find any, buy a fistful and send me some because they both work and cast. Last year, when I was caught without them in my kit, I created some eyeballs with heavy mono burned at each end to form a ball. Then I folded some deer hair for a tail and some other strands to make shrimp horns/prawn feelers and put some glue on the back to create a shell. It was a funny little critter of which no two were the same, but they all worked. Shrimp make stripers crazy. Keep in mind this important consideration: It is unnatural to fish with pink-colored shrimp because they are opaque to light brown in real life. Tiers whose only sighting of shrimp is from hors d'oeuvres at a party are mindful of artists who depict the bottom of the ocean with red lobsters—clear evidence that they have never been there. These animals are only pink, or red, after they are cooked. I also think that shrimp swim backward, which sounds to me like we tie them facing the wrong way. Wait a minute, I hear funny music, do you?

CINDER WORMS

These are easy to tie because anytime something does not work, how it is tied is irrelevant. The idea is to have a fuzzy marine animal with a black head and orange body under an inch long. Do not call me when cinders are hatching out in your pet estuary because chances

These shrimp patterns all bring bass to the table. They love shrimp.

are I am already denying any knowledge of the event. Worm hatches can be the most frustrating episode in fly fishing the striper surf because the stripers are plowing around noisily and your offering, competing with one million on a poor hatch and one billion on a normal one, has little chance of being taken with so much of the real animal darting about. A lineside sloshes over here, but by the time you cast to where it was, it is gone and another is sloshing so close to your waders you feel its tail. You can of course double your chances by throwing two flies at once with a dropper, as you have zero likelihood of ever catching two bass at once. On the other hand, two times nothing is still nothing.

There is so much junk science regarding species of cinder worm, the most likely timing for a swarm, and suitable water temperatures that the subject of debunking the worm fairy-lore is bigger than the known body of knowledge on the worms themselves. For instance, I read somewhere that they won't swarm until the water is 60 degrees. My wife and I enjoyed a worm hatch in early June 2003 in Rhode Island, an unusually cold spring, when the water was 53. Observers say that worm hatches are a spring thing but I have been in them so thick, swarming so prodigiously in August, that we had acres of bass around us for only an occasional take. Opinion on all cinder worm activity is largely based on those occasions when the person talking happened to be among them. I can offer no concrete advice for dealing with this situation except to say that you are certainly not going to stay at home waiting for such a hatch anyway. Like me, you are going to go fishing when you can, as often as you can. Bass will still feed, and sometimes blitz, with or without the worms. And you should have a few worm imitations in your vest for that occasion.

CLOUSER MINNOWS

This family of flies has added dramatically to the list of effective fly types that makes up the striper arsenal. The large barbell of beady eyes that are distinctive in Clousers cause the fly to ride point-up. My introduction to these was an embarrassing situation that I would prefer not to confess here. Try to forget about it after you read it.

I was fishing an outflow in Rhode Island with a fellow and his twelve-year-old son, Scotty, when they were catching five school stripers to my one. Anyway, Scotty seemed to feel sorry for me and offered me a Clouser, which I promptly refused because I am too important to accept flies from kids. After a while of their both five-to-oneing me, Scotty, the little rascal, said, "Sure you don't want a fly, Frank?"

Anyway, just to keep him quiet, I accepted a Clouser with black deer hair dressing and turned the situation to five to five. This gets better in a variation of the big eyes riding hook-up on something else.

OWENS VELVET EEL

Fly shops are candy stores, and I head for the patterns they offer first thing whenever visiting one. Usually I will buy anything that interests me so that I can copy it at home at the vise. Like you, I have also done this with flies presented to me on trout streams. We all like to tie our own. This particular time I spotted a sand eel imitation that was perfect in size and proportion to the real animal. Made from velvet tubing, white body with dark dorsal, green fading in gradient down the sides, it had those big, beady eyes used in the Clouser. This one was a no-brainer, as I caught bass with it the first time out and proceeded to tie up a bunch.

Quite by accident, while foraging for more tubing at a fly shop in Connecticut, I raved about the pattern to the clerk there, who promptly told me that the pattern's initiator, Brian Owens, worked there. "Have you tried it in black?" he asked.

"No," I answered, "I didn't know it was offered in black."

"Black is way better," he said.

And it was, and I never again fished with a Velvet Eel that was the color of a sand eel. Why a black version would take more bass remains a mystery. I can only say that it might be the stronger silhouette that black casts while night fishing—except that black is also better after sunrise. I have tied both color variations of the Owens flies with weightless pearl chain eyes that ride hook-point-down for use in riffling with the Portland hitch and done just as well.

We all do it but I have to mention the risk in marrying a pattern. I was so impressed with the black Owens that I put together a bunch of them for our son, Dick, and the girls. The time I gave them the flies, we were fly fishing along the Maine coastline in daylight off a point known to produce regularly at that particular stage of tide. I was certain we would clean up, but when it became evident that nothing was going to happen our daughter Susan put on a Quigley Baby Angel and hooked up right away. When the rest of us changed over, we all hooked fish. Here, at this place in this time, the marvelous Owens Velvet Eel was a dud. That's why we have fly cases.

Rubber "Flies"

The way the theory goes, a big reason why flies work so well is that the materials within the fly have life of their own. The stripping action causes the fly materials, wispy and flexible, to pulsate. The materials in the fly enjoy a small activity under the light pressure of the currents that do their part in this, and the fly enjoys a "bugginess" as a result. I wouldn't dispute it because fly fishers have all seen the results repeated with any number of patterns. However, there are some things that cannot be replicated with traditional materials. Some shapes are best molded. It is often possible to make something at the molding bench that is so small—a lure, really—it has to be presented with fly-fishing methods. Once a "lure" falls below a quarter ounce in saltwa-

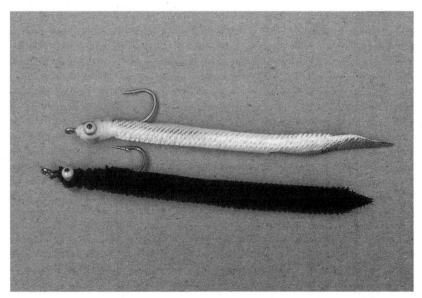

The Owens Velvet Eel has been my latest "secret weapon." Fly love affairs never quit.

ter fishing, it is impossible to cast; any heavier than that, and fly casting is not an option either. Thus, the choices are often dictated by the heaviness of the artificial. We fly cast what we cannot deliver by spinning or baitcasting. It is that simple.

A great example of an effective lure that is too light for casting and nearly too heavy for fly fishing is the smaller-sized red-gill. This molded rubber sand eel replica of British origin made its reputation in the States as a teaser when other heavier items were utilized as casting weights—say, plugs or tins. In the smaller sizes, if distance fly casting is not required, red-gills simulate sand eels and sperling nicely. The action generated by the swimmer plate tail really turns on saltwater gamefish. Nevertheless, 4½-inch red-gills weighing one-seventh of an ounce are about as heavy as can be fished as lone flies—and lighter is better in this case.

Some of the rubber worms sold in bulk for use in freshwater bass fishing effectively simulate mature sea worms—either blood worms or clam worms. These worms are commonly fished live on the bottom and take huge stripers. What some tiers do is put the hook in a fly-tying vise and tie a small underwrap of Danville Flat Waxed Nylon, common to fly tiers, with your bobbin for, say, half an inch, then whip-finish the wrap. Dab some superglue on the wrap and slide the rubber worm over the gooey underwrap; it dries within seconds. This holds the molded rubber lure in place on the hook for much longer, and helps it stand up to hits and casting forces.

The Little Baits

A number of companies have gone to molding small critters—grubs, worms, crickets, hoppers, and, of course, shrimp. These replicate the real thing nicely and would have to appeal to gamefish. (Burke Flex-O-Lures in Traverse City, Michigan, had a delightful line of molded rubber insects that I have used since I was a boy, but I can no longer find them.) Grass shrimp are particularly exciting because they are fed upon by just about everything willing to visit an estuary. I can't count the number of times I have found stripers in some backwater, eating shrimp, and when they do so, they can be very selective. Grass shrimp, rarely over an inch long, are way too small for easy simulation with a suitable hook for saltwater gamefish, so you are forced to make some

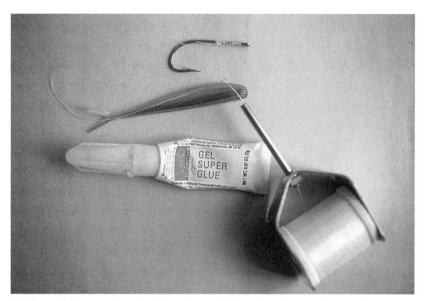

This Fin-S fish turns their heads. A base of thread and superglue cinches it.

hard choices between what will make them hit and a hook that will hold them. Still, a rubber shrimp casting should be used and stripers, weakfish, and even blues will take it readily. Lure makers are coming up with new molded soft plastic products all the time. Most are being developed for use with various designs of leadhead delivery system. Lifelike castings of shrimp, crawdads, small baitfish, along with new animals we've never heard of—"Mag Squidzits" or "Saucy Shads"— with a liberal number of legs, feelers, and tentacles are often small enough to be thrown by fly fishers. The weightless presentation, in spite of going against original intent, is a far more natural, more effective, option.

We often see people fishing in tidewaters with small lures that have leadheads up front for the dual purpose of providing casting weight and getting down in the currents. If you think about it, the more weight is involved, the more the offering moves through the water like an overloaded stick. It is functional in some situations and I do it too, but anytime a small lure is permitted to drift naturally without weight in light currents, it offers a better, more natural simulation because with neutral buoyancy it will slide naturally between the pulses you apply. A dead drift works better, is more natural, when the offering is not encumbered by weight—a fly.

Lunker City—Molded Rubber Lures of All Sizes

A modern striper artificial often used with casting tackle in the striper surf is the Fin-S fish. These are thrown at sizes up to 9 inches both with lead and weightless. Further, at the other end of the size spectrum Lunker City offers a 2½-inch model Fin-S fish, which is perfect for mounting on either a 1/0 or 1 hook (34007 stainless). This is a little sweetie pie when drifted on the end of a fly line. Plus, the other fishers with casting equipment cannot fish it, which some nights can bust chops in a big way. They're easy to cast, weigh a mere tenth of an ounce, and all gamefish munch them—even fluke. What I like about rubber is that if the lure/fly is taken and the gamester is not pricked too badly, the texture of the rubber often has them coming right back for a second hit, which gives you another chance. Price is no object when something works in the striper surf, but you can buy a package of twenty for a trifle over three dollars. Use the same nylon underwrap and superglue assembly described above for rubber worms. It is an awesome lure that can be cast with "fly-fishing" equipment and you can call it anything you want—fly or lure—because the fish don't care.

Hook Size

Hook sizes for the flies I use in striper fishing run from 1 to 3/0. Any larger hook becomes unwieldy for casting. One reason why we have to limit the overall weight of any fly is that in order for the hook to be in harmony with the fly size—big flies call for big hooks—you end up with a spinning lure instead of a fly. Creators of overly large bunker and alewife patterns should keep this in mind. Most of my patterns are wound to 1/0 hooks, which seems to be a size that both handles well for casting and is large enough for two-handed stripers. Of my favorite flies, I make certain that I keep at least some 2/0 and 3/0 models around for when I am fishing among big bass—say, over 40 inches, which is 25 pounds. Fish of that size, and you will run into them, can take a softball in their mouths. These bigger hooks provide a greater penetration, which hopefully will improve hooking qualities of your fly choice on big linesides. I hasten to add that you could handle any striper that swims with the size 1.

The rush to imitate every marine creature at the fly tier's bench was, I am certain, inspired by the desire to sell flies. The variations available in crab patterns best illustrates this, and wild stories about the finding of selective striped bass that fell for juvenile crabs crept slowly on the bottom would require another volume. Similarly, this has also been done with baby squid—big glass eyes, tentacles trailing, pink/opaque coloration. I'm sure these creations are meant more to fool anglers, but who wants to take the chance? Every fly gets its opportunity to be the most important one in your vest.

Riffle Hitch for Attention

By definition a riffle hitch is a means of tying your fly to the leader in a way that causes it to plane on the surface. Through the use of the right knot, the wet fly can be made to ride the surface tension, leaving an attention-getting V-wake as it travels the currents without the help of flotation. The principle that causes the fly to "riffle" is the same as that which forces a side planer while trolling to move outboard of a vessel's wake—moving water.

To tie the hitch, fasten it with a routine clinch knot. Then throw a pair of overhand knots around the throat of the fly. Be careful not to miss the fly, as an overhand knot will reduce leader strength by half; when not allowed to tighten upon itself, there is no loss of strength.

While I wish I could tell you that I invented the riffle hitch, the truth is I first learned about it during the striper moratorium while Atlantic salmon fishing in the early 1980s. New to the game in those days, I had no experience with customary salmon-fishing knots. What I used to do was fasten the fly to my leader in the same manner I had become accustomed to with trout and stripers. I didn't know that I was doing something different.

Why would I think so when I caught as many salmon as most and a lot more than many? Then one morning one of the regulars, a Mainer, cautioned me that this was not a riffling river and that I was wasting my time fishing that way. Faking it, I dared not ask what the heck "riffling" was and just kept right on fishing the way I knew how.

The subject came up again on the same river a year later with a different person. Only this time I asked a few questions and this guy admonished, "You know darn well what I'm talking about. Nobody has their fly running the surface that way, takes the kind of salmon that you take, without knowing why."

I had never known why. I had never intended to "riffle" because at the time, I never even knew it was an option. Just lucky, I guess.

Why, then, is this means of securing a wet fly used in salmon fishing when it has had no application elsewhere? Books say that when eighteenth-century British naval officers arrived at the Maritimes' Portland Creek, they resorted to salmon fishing because there was little else happening. Finding a stash of salmon flies from a previous vessel, it was noted that the snelled gut leaders built into the fly dressings had begun to separate and become unreliable. Thus the sailors threw a "Portland hitch" around the fly's throat to deal with concerns about leaders pulling from the flies. When their offerings rode the surface of the rivers leaving a V-wake—caused by the new hitch—they experienced a greater number of takes than they had ever seen before, and a methodology was born. Salmoneers have

The Riffle Hitch.

used it here and there ever since. However, I have never seen riffling done other than for salmon.

One reason why it took hold in river fishing is current. In order for the fly to slide on top, water has to be moving past. The effort is wasted in deadwaters or most open beaches. However, in inlets, or some prominent stick-out points during full tide, where the sea is humping past, there is sufficient current to push the fly to the top and make it work. We all know that current is something favored by bass, so there is a nice marriage of conditions here that accommodates riffling the fly.

When a fly is attached at the throat, it riffles a lot better than when simply clinch-knotted. To some degree I had been riffling as early as fifteen years before salmon fishing, but I wasn't doing it consciously—partly because it was dark most of the time, partly because I didn't know enough to look, and partly because the other considerations were often not in place. There are things you can do to help a fly riffle better.

Along with the need for current and proper attachment, sparsely dressed flies ride better with fewer materials to pull them under. Smaller hooks also riffle more readily. In addition, because this is a topwater mission, a floating line and shorter leader are recommended.

Atlantic salmon behavior is a poor model for comparisons to other fish. Salmon do not feed when in rivers, and volumes have been written that have sought to explain their outrageous behavior. With stripers, on the other hand, feeding *is* the mission. It then is a case of getting their attention—having them *see* your fly, and having them sort it out as more vulnerable than other baitfish. I suspect that both sand eel and sperling behaviors contribute to how well the technique works because they both often rest at an angle with their heads in the surface tension. At times all baitfish will break the surface either when disturbed or when moving upcurrent. There are other ways to leave a V-wake.

Rigging Up

This is where you pack your parachute. If there is anything wrong with how you set up your equipment, the striper of your dreams is going to tell you. If it happens to you, don't tell anyone you have been reading my books. Let's start at the reel and move out toward the striper's jaw.

The surface microfinish of my fly spools is a click short of glass in smoothness. Nothing that you do to attach your backing to that reel is going to pin it down. It will hold with almost any knot, but if not attached correctly, the entire backing and fly line will rotate as a unit. There may be other ways, but what I have done since first confronted with this as a young man is tie the backing securely without regard for rotation, then tape the knot and line wrap with at least two turns of plastic or electrical tape. Once the attachment is taped down, subsequent turns of line on top of the tape will secure the tape and, consequently, the knot. I have never had the backing and fly line rotate as a unit with this method of securing the backing.

When settling on the amount of backing, be sure to put as much of it on as you can without interfering with the space needed for the fly line. Usually I look at another similar spool and guess about the amount needed; I can come pretty close while still allowing for the fly line. I like 200 yards, although it is unlikely you will ever run out of backing in the run of your best bass. Try to remove the coating of the bottom of the line for about 3 inches, so as to have enough of the fly line's base braid exposed for a safe knot. Attach the two—the backing and fly line—with a simple blood knot, where each line is wrapped around the other at least six turns then passed through the loop, the two tag ends passing in opposite directions. When cinching these up, always moisten them. You want this to be a small, strong knot because it is the one you are going to feel hitting the guides when a run takes you into the backing. Probably the most dangerous place in your setup, failure here will cost you a fish and a fly line.

Attaching the first piece of your leader to the front of the fly line, use a nail knot to connect the heavy mono to the fly line. After that, successive pieces of ever-thinner leader material can be attached—50, 40, 30, 20—each section 2 feet long and the last piece, the tippet, 3 feet so as to provide material for fly changes. I always carry a leader roll of 12-pound tippet for those nights when I am confronted with selectivity and have concerns about leader-shy stripers. Leaders usually end up around rod length. For faster-sinking lines, I shorten up all the sections to keep the fly down with the line. I attach the fly with an improved clinch knot.

When you open a fly line from any of the fly-line companies, you will find illustrated instructions of the various knots used in setting up. If you are good with knots, you can follow these instructions quite easily.

Equipment in Order of Importance

1. Fly line
2. Rigging
3. Fly reel
4. Rod choice
5. Fly choice
6. Leader—length and strength
7. Backing—length and strength

3
Topography and Choosing Water

Effective shore fishing is a study in topography. As a surfcaster, you are looking for geology that thwarts the movement of water in a way that will accelerate it. A large open bay with an island that constricts the movement of tide will force the water past it on both sides with more force. A point that juts out into the open sea will usually have water rushing past. Every change in the geology of the land commonly reflects some change below the sea surface. If you can see the land, you can generally read the bottom of the ocean. If you can read the structure, you can read the water.

The structure-forming mix that creates favored locations for gamefish is the result of a season's winds, the combined effect of a year's storms, and the magnitude and therefore intensity of local tides. I say *local* because there are profound differences in tidal exchange between many points of the Striper Coast. For instance, during spring tides in Rhode Island the difference in water level is 4 feet, whereas only 50 miles east the same tide produces an 11-foot tidal exchange. A consequence of this is that stronger tide rips make up where there is the most water. These rips create more structure where the observant shore fisher can seek stripers.

That is not to say that you should favor a location because of its greater tidal exchange; nor does it mean that Montauk Point is inferior to Race Point on Cape Cod because the rips are stronger. All I seek to point out here is that current and structure, with their subsequent relationship, are relative to the surrounding waters. Indeed, many locations enjoy angling fame more for social reasons than for the actual fishing. One reason why Cape Cod is good is because people are allowed to fish there.

Knowing what kinds of shore appeals to bass takes the guesswork out of striper hunting.

Let's get back to geology. In the spin of our precious planet, the Gulf Stream pumps north-northeast to the Gulf of Maine before crossing the Atlantic. This warm water back-eddies to form Cape Cod before heading over to England to secure a milder climate there. The Gulf Stream has created a marvelous sandbar in the Cape, having washed away the lighter material of the Elizabethan chain in that process. I have been in the Gulf Stream and seen the foam that forms at its very edge. They say that even the water temperature is different on each side of this demarcation line. Similarly, but on a much smaller scale, I have been in the actual so-called Race that borders Outer Cape Cod where the water forms a discernible line within its movement. It's not just the current of Race Point minor that does this, but also the current sweeping the entire Outer Cape, as though it were an exaggerated shadow of the land. Moreover, below the surface, depth readings plummet sufficiently for the reader to envision a virtual wall of sand below that is over 100 feet. Regardless, I talk of this enlarged view of topography to emphasize the relativity of all structure.

Reading Beaches

The beaches from which we fish are mere microcosms of what I have talked about here so far. A 1-foot drop-off has as much significance to the caster on a small beach as that 100-foot drop of the Race. The water that broke over a sandbar and then rushes back seaward through a small opening, while way less in volume and spirit, is as influential in its own way as Long Island Sound's tidal exchange. An inconsequential tidal creek is just another Hudson River of less magnitude. They all play a role in dictating the movement of stripers. The caster who knows water and why it hurries this way or that is not working from a list of hot spots that he read in a magazine. Rather, he is applying his sense of reading the water, his knowledge of the hydrolysis of moving water. Of course, anyone who has even a slight mastery of beach reading is sure to find a crowd fishing when he gets where he's going. There are people who read the water that way and do fine. Nevertheless, the subtleties of the skill still hold many yet undiscovered hot spots that yield only one hour a day. The timing of them all is the key.

Beaches change because no season is ever the same in its summary of storms and powerful winds. It is possible to have a place where the bass gather but are only vulnerable at low tide because when the tide is full, the configuration on the bottom is not contributing to the water's movement. Then, once the tide has fallen enough, the harmless curve in the sand begins to influence the water where waves break over an outer bar, slide into a hole, then rush out of the opening in the center of the hole. Sometimes there are sloughs at both ends of the hole where any bass that have ventured into the shallows swim with the moving water because they sense a safety in water that has a place to go. They will gather at the opening of the hole to lie in the current facing the shore, or they will collect where the sloughs dump into the hole. Sometimes, when the water is down enough, they might hold in the deeper corners of this hole. And once the tide is low, they will slip out the only deeper opening to look for another cycle of time and tide.

The wise surfcaster guards his beach-reading honey hole for another season. Nonetheless, the experienced one knows that chances are it will not be there next season. So it is not the actual hole that is important. It is having the knowledge to find it and how to fish it that is the talent. I have known many of these places and have come to appreciate that they only sometimes yield for a second year. Maybe that is why it is a mistake to marry a beach; you will not know the place another time.

On Nauset Beach on Cape Cod there are some years when the entire beach is punctuated by an endless mix of bars, sloughs, deep cuts, and holes. I fish these at low tide because that is when they can be seen. Other years there is little to go by, and the lack of luster of that shore does not inspire serious fishing. It is deep and straight at high tide, shallow and straight at low. Nobody ever said that fishing the beach was easy or reliable.

If you bathe on Rhode Island's South Shore you might discover there is a slight drop-off of less than a foot—it is called the rut—just seaward of where the waves break. Some years it is hard to find, and others it can be located easily. Legend has it, and I like *legend* because it dignifies uncertainty, that the big bass there swim the rut when engaged in either migration or feeding movements. I don't know if the rut acts as a barrier for their surf play, as is commonly believed, but I have caught many big bass at the end of my retrieve, where the waves break. Moreover, I have often seen schools of bass working bait where the waves slide back, at the rough location of the rut, and have taken them by casting down the beach with a sinking line. It seems that gamefish adjust to water and structure conditions so as to suit their foraging needs.

For instance, there is a stretch on Cape Cod, from Wood End/Long Point clear to Race Point Light, where the beach drops off so fast that there are 15 feet of water under your cast—no structure, nothing to read or work over. Yet the bass will often dig or forage right where the waves pan at the water's edge. There is dry sand 3 feet from where their backs are out of the water while digging for sand eels. If you forget, or never knew, you can flush them out of the surf when you walk up to them—the grinding sand from your boots alerts them, and they

Surfy open beaches call for the use of a stripping basket and close line mending.

will scoot off with a sudden popping sound. However, they usually don't go far but stop and lay up within casting distance. Or you can wait, or look for another one, because this is group behavior. Even the ones you flush come back to resume digging and feeding.

Some parts of the Striper Coast have bars that run perpendicular to the shore. At high tide there is not much to see; about all there is of it is well below the surface. However, at low water a caster can wade out to the ends of these finger bars that, at this stage, are obstacles shore runners have to go around. Some such bars enjoy deep drop-offs on one side, and the bass will lie in them. Near the Cape's Highland Light, I have found the corners on the left (north) sides of the finger bars to be cut deeply and, for some reason, hiding baitfish when none can be found elsewhere. Often there is a bass or two holding in these spots that will take, providing you do not go looking for them with a light, or create vibrations or grinding sand noise with your boots.

Once you get a feel for how they are acting, it is possible to confine your efforts to just the places that have garnered their interest. For example, if you are catching only on the left side of bar ends on drop-offs, forgo testing the right sides or the bar corners and just fish the terrain that is producing for you. Of course, once the tide changes, you might find it necessary to shift to the right edges because the stripers are responding to the water's direction change. Like dogs riding in a vehicle, bass want the movement—current, in this case—in their faces.

Rocky Shores

Rocky shores offer more structure, more hiding places for forage, and more permanence. It takes severe weather to change a stony shore, and places known to appeal to bass can be revisited year after year with a reasonable expectation of activity. Many rocky shorelines enjoy prominent points that obstruct enough for stripers to pass sufficiently close that you can target them from shore. Coves, in this case an indentation between two points, often hold trapped bait, so it might be necessary to fish it all.

There are problems with rocky coastlines that are more difficult for the fly fisher to overcome than those fishing with a pool cue and 70-pound-test lines. Rocks mean barnacles, mussels, oysters, and varieties of marine life that will damage your line. Such shores are often dangerous for landing trophy stripers. Nothing is more distressing than having a huge cow bass lying there belly-up and exhausted in the surf and not being able to reach her without risking your life. You must not select casting platforms that are too high above the water unless you are close enough to suitable landing sites.

I cannot complete this discussion on stones without reminding all of you that what few deaths occur surfcasting are frequently on rocky shores where the hapless fisher finds himself in big crashing waves that will bounce him off the stones. The only option is to swim out, but that presents a whole new set of problems.

Jetties are a variation on the rocky shore option with the added complication of being popular with other fishers. You will usually find that jetty fishing with a fly rod is best done alone. Even then, be mindful of where your stripping falls, as I have ruined a good fly line that tangled in the stones beneath me and was no longer usable after I recovered it. (The solution, which I don't like, is a stripping basket.) Jetties provide an obstacle for bass to move past, a change in the configuration of the land, and a corner to corral baitfish. Usually the nook

Jetties and rocky shores appeal to stripers, but they can be tough fly fishing.

where wind-driven waves collect has an edge. All jetties in Rhode Island flank inlets that are famous for their fishing.

Big Bays

Large protected bays offer a variety of all the structure enumerated above without the surf complicating your fishing efforts. Many bays—Barnegat, Raritan, Peconic, Narragansett, Pleasant Bay on the Cape, Boston Harbor, and Great Bay in New Hampshire, to name only some—would almost give the illusion of large lakes, were it not for their tidal activity. Sandy areas shallow enough for wading, points at their openings or distributed inside, small outflows, river mouths, narrows with accelerating current, provide micro representations of the larger points in geography mentioned earlier. The key is change that creates moving water. Most important, just because some of these places are small does not mean that fishing potential is diminished. Striped bass were spawned in water barely deep enough to cover their mother's back, and they feel comfortable in small water as a result. The elemental fury of the sea is really the only thing missing.

I would never hesitate to work any bay if I thought there were enough bait to appeal to stripers, or knew of a run of fish, or had some fanciful desire to go there simply for the geographic advantage of it. Still, escape from storms is one of the most richly important reasons to fish these places. How many times in a life of fly fishing the Striper Coast is your favorite spot blown out by a nor'easter or a hurricane? The wise angler who chooses his spot for the protection it affords goes fishing in spite of the weather. Thus, when the coast is wild with mare's tails, foam bouncing off the wave tops, silt suspended in the booming surf, all punctuated by what the beach boys once called "good vibrations," you fish while your counterpart on that dismal shore laments.

Flats

Most "flats fishing" is carried out from boats, and the subject does not deserve the attention in a surf-fishing treatment that it might otherwise. There are of course some flats where the wading angler has the opportunity to cover large areas of shallow water that often hold bait and lure stripers to them as a result. Most of the shallow areas that would qualify are adjacent to deeper channels that lead the bass in under the cover of darkness. You have to know your way around these areas—know the location of drop-offs, be acquainted with horizon landmarks, probably carry a compass, and be ever-conscious of the tide. Fog is a very real hazard for a person who is a long way from shore without the safety of a boat. Flats fishing without a boat is a very dangerous choice in this list of types of shoreline. A rising tide is very sneaky.

Small "flats" like those on the salt ponds of Rhode Island's South Shore or New Jersey's back bays are not that dangerous. In contrast, the Joppa Flats on the mouth of the Merrimack River has strong currents; fly fishers there often have to go over their waders to get back to shore. The Brewster Flats in Cape Cod Bay, a location that is routinely enveloped in fog, often hosts anglers who are a mile or more from safety while engaged in wild, distracting bass fishing. It is dream fishing that gets people into trouble; I would not go there without a rubber duck under my arm, maybe two.

A great deal of attention has been given flats fishing in recent years on the Striper Coast. I believe that some professionals have sought to re-create—Florida-ize, if you will—striper fishing here in the North in the hope of re-creating the boom in angling tourism enjoyed in the Keys. There are better ways to shore fish for stripers.

Inlets—The Striper Holes

By definition, an inlet is any opening to the sea that connects to an estuary or river. I place no size limitations on this interpretation. I have fished inlets that were nothing more than brooks about 8 feet wide; to really stretch the examples, even the Cape Cod Canal is an inlet for Buzzards Bay on the west end and Cape Cod Bay on the east. Be it a brook or a 700-foot-wide ditch, I have caught stripers in both that had gone to face the current and wait for a handout. If Long Island Sound qualifies as an inlet, then it would explain why Montauk is so famous for stripers and why the Fishers Island Race smokes with linesides and other gamefish. Why are inlets striper holes, you ask? Because nearly all the marine life-forms upon which bass feed are nurtured in these tidal marshes. Water moves, providing oxygen-rich breathing.

As a consequence, bass do not go to them to rest, they go there to forage lazily in the moving water. All estuaries are smaller than the open ocean and heat up more quickly from the warmth of the sun. I think bass go to them for the moving water alone, but I believe they find inlets through the scent of bait and through the change in water temperature. Also, the heat provides a better environment for the incubation of all wildlife.

Consequently, were I thrust into a strange territory where I had never fished, I would use even the crudest map I could find and start looking for an inlet, an outflow from an estuarine pond or river mouth. Inlets are so basic to striper hunting that when I did the research for my third book, *Striper Hot Spots: The 100 Top Surfcasting Locations from New Jersey to Maine*, I found that two-thirds of the most popular surfcasting places on the Striper Coast were inlets. Many of the other spots enjoyed their location in the book because of the influence of inlets nearby. Therefore the dynamics of how they work, how you should fish them, and what few others ever learn are among the most critical in the grocery list of things-to-know in your striper repertoire.

Inlets or estuarine openings are my favorite water.

INLET DYNAMICS

Estuaries fill with a rising tide then empty on the ebb, creating two sets of tidal conditions. Formula inlet fishing usually relies upon a falling tide as the most popular for drawing gamefish to the currents that form where the inlet spills into the sea. Surfcasters will gather in large numbers at the most seaward edge of the opening of the more important inlets. In order to provide fairness to all, a rotation is often established where a given number of casters take turns moving through; this gives everyone who is fishing in harmony a chance to fish. If there are five fishable positions and ten casters, five are in line waiting for their turn. An outcome of the rotation system is that everyone is very social. If you go into the situation with the right attitude, you can both make some friends and learn more about fishing in general—and that inlet in particular. I also like to watch how others are fishing so as to know if anything is being missed. What anglers do is feed their floating lures into the current for as far seaward as the current will take them, allowing them to swing through the current, then retrieve and repeat the process. Inlets, as popular as they are, usually draw large crowds so that you have no chance of fishing alone, and even less at fly fishing. The fishing lasts until the tide slackens, the sunrise ends the action, or all present are certain that no gamefish are going to show. The fly fisher is not likely to have access to this situation in the more significant—more crowded—spots. Still, it is possible to work the edges of these places, or position yourself far enough upstream to avoid those crowds. In addition, many smaller inlets are overlooked that provide reliable collections of stripers each night during a falling tide. Never think that because an outflow is small, it will appeal only to schoolies. Big fish eat the same things and feed the same way.

Of less significance, and getting less attention from the angling public as a result, is the fishing of these places during a *rise* in tide. Keep in mind that all the water that goes out has to come in too, and bass will still face the current on the incoming. However, at this time there is more room for fly fishing. The competent observer must determine how the rips form up for this rising stage of tide because everything about the place is different. Usually, but not necessarily, the waterway's most seaward edge appeals on the drop, while the inlet's most inland edge is the best on the rise. The rise causes fish to be drawn from the estuary, and the drop lures them from the larger ocean. If there are points along the way, there will be eddies off those points that might hold a bass or two. Naturally, any location that pays off tonight is one for you to remember because it is a lie that is popular with the linesides at that particular stage of tide. They too, like salmon and trout, take a shine to certain kinds of water. Nor is the study of a particular inlet so simple that you need only know two tidal situations. Sometimes an inlet offers holding water that changes with the increase or decrease in current. Every little thing that you notice should be remembered if you want consistency and intimacy with a hot spot. Even deadwater, the four slack tides per day, can be important. Here's why.

Once an outflow goes dead at slack tide—high or low—the feeding opportunity in that particular situation is over for the foragers. Some may drop back into the open sea, while others may prepare to take up new feeding stations in anticipation of the incoming, and a kind of musical chairs occurs accordingly. It is the time when all the fish that were holding in parts of the neighborhood unexposed to angling might pass. These could be fish that were too far out for a drifted

Schoolies like this one will run backwaters under the cover of darkness.

plug or were holding on the bottom too deep to see it or to take it. You do not ever want to be eating your lunch or scratching while waiting for the tide to change, because slack is a good time. For the fly fisherman, it is a chance to work water that might even have been too strong earlier, and also a time when a battle with a good striper is not made more severe by the currents of an hour before. Fish it all.

When taking all this into account, inlets are very tide dependent, and you have to know which tide is going to provide the best opportunity. Having said that, and I do want to say it all in something as important as this, if the buggers were around on the drop, there is a good chance they will be there on the rise. The tide dependence of inlets requires an understanding of timing water movement in a particular location.

Due to the difference in size between the two containers—ocean and estuary—they do not fill and empty on the same timing as the actual high and low tide that you see on the chart. What occurs is a lag between when the tide is high in the front, what you read on the chart, and when it is high in the estuary—lag. Thus the tide might be high in the ocean outside the Harbor of Refuge in Rhode Island at midnight, but not slack or high inside the harbor until 1 or 2 AM. The lag there happens to be an hour or two later, and the actual outflow will not begin until the harbor is higher than the dropping ocean. Various inlets have different lag times, and you need to become familiar with the ones you frequent. You don't want to get there too early if you are going to fish the drop or you will be sitting on the rocks waiting for the tide to start flowing out and building the fish-drawing currents. The night is long enough as it is. Conversely, incoming tide will occur after ocean low tide once the outside is higher than the water level of the estuary—again, because of lag.

STANDARDIZED INLET TACTICS

There are always those with other ideas about how they want to fish. They may want to drift eels or fish the bottom or liveline bunker. Nevertheless, in order to keep harmony in the situation, it is better if everyone is doing the same thing.

The longer the tide falls, the more time the situation has had to lure fish to the opening. Thus, I would always make a point of timing my night, taking lag into account, so as to be there during the tail end of the drop while it is still dark. Also—and remember that you heard this here—when the inlet currents are slacking, everything that was in front that could not be reached by all those gorillas you were fishing with is about to change positions. The fish could be close to you and they have not been exposed to any of what was presented. It is a good time.

When water is flowing out of an inlet, the sea tide running along the beach will bend the lines of infusion so that the current ends up with a hook in it, yielding to the force outside. Bass often rest inside this hook for relief from the current while still able to pluck from what is going by. However, the side of the flow that the hook is on—the one downtide of the ocean current—changes once the ocean tide changes. Moreover, your inlet will still be falling outward in spite of the ocean beginning its rise, so there is no indication in your fore that this change has taken place. Thus, the hook that was on the left side of the flow and its eddy is now on the right, and the guys who are on the right side of the outflow have more action than those who are on the left. It is another outgrowth of lag, the difference in tide between the inlet and the ocean.

Unless others are fly fishing this spot, stay as far away from other fishers as possible. Work as far up, and as way up, as you can in order to allow enough time to get that fish in. Anglers always seem to think that bass won't run a creek or a tidal run, but remember that they were spawned in shallow water after dark. Stripers are way less oceanic than bluefish, so don't worry about the back pond's ability to provide good fishing; it is often the part of an inlet that is overlooked by others, and many regulars will be distressed at seeing you there.

Anytime an inlet has been reliable during the drop, and usually crowded as a result, there will be a percentage of the same fish in the currents of the incoming tide. This is a situation that calls for some discretion, but few anglers either feel comfortable on the incoming or are willing to fish both. They stay with what they know and you fish alone, which is fine with me.

In addition to crowds, because moorings are often inside those estuaries, inlets can suffer from excessive boat traffic; hence gamefish depart to a more subdued environment. The more boats that go by, the longer we all have to wait for things to quiet. Weekends or early morning this traffic can shut off the fishing entirely. Daylight usually ends the action even if there have been fish all night—usually.

We all find it necessary to use a light to change flies, inspect bait-fish, or get past a nasty spot. Remember, though, that in the smaller inlets—and bear in mind that I have fished outflows that were small brooks—indiscreet use of lights sends bass out into deep, unreachable water. These are wild fish programmed for survival.

BE CAREFUL OUT THERE

Most inlets—say, from Jersey north to Monomoy—are flanked by jetties, which means that inlet fishing is jetty fishing. As a rule, you can go off the same way you went on. However, from the Outer Cape north, skipping Boston, then to Maine again, many inlets are wild without the flanking of jetties. Water in greater tidal exchange shifts the sands, bars, sloughs, crossings, and general structure. The spot you were so intimate with last season is way different from what you remember. It is here that lag will get you.

Typically, you feel safe on that bar a quarter mile from the beach because you can see the water falling from the inlet. The tide is going out, right? In contrast, what is really happening is that while the back pond falls, the front is rising and filling that deep cut you strained to the top of your waders when you came out on the bar. What you can do after you say good-bye to all your friends with your cell phone is remove your waders, tie them at the bottom, and use them for water wings to get back to the beach, assuming the fog has not obscured your route. Night, tide, fog, and lack of familiarity are the nasty ingredients of the mortician's brew.

WORKING THE WATER

Let's look at the water column. When we appreciate that inlet dynamics are current dependent, it is necessary to understand how bass hold in these currents. Two places permit them to hold with less effort: the bottom and the bank edges. Therefore, you will get more hits with a sinking line that is presented high enough upcurrent so that it is down deep when it begins to go under tension. Once it tightens up, it will likely be ambushed against the bank or while you are stripping in. In some locations, bottom rocks will create neutral hydros that bass will hold in. If intimate enough with the run, you can go back to these and take fish with regularity. Some "lies" seem always to have bass waiting for tidbits to drift by, and my wife and I often joke about

Tide out on a Maine fjord. But after the rise and with darkness, it is all different.

who gets the first cast there. Often, after having fought and released a few fish, the notion that we have stuck all that was there comes through as action declines. Eventually we move on upcurrent or down or even move the buggy for another location. But after a while, and I cannot count how many times we have done this, if we come back and work the spot the same way all over again, more stripers—presumably different ones—are back. You wonder what characteristic the spot has that so appeals to them, but the main things are that both you and the bass come back for another meeting.

I work productive, promising water as methodically as I can to be certain that my fly passes in a set of parallel arcs that cover every reachable foot of the place. With this kind of moving water, a simple dead drift under tension is your best way to fish; it is not necessary to impart action to the fly. I will throw a short cast, pull a foot off the reel, and repeat until I have reached the limit of what I can handle without getting a casting hernia. Then, with that same amount of line out, I will step downcurrent to swing another pass on the place and keep going until I get to the top of my waders. It is possible with this method to envision having cut an arc with my fly through the entire reachable portion of the estuarine opening. In the process of working the water, if you feel the slightest suspicious movement on your fly, you have raised a fish. Often, they have risen for your fly but aborted the take for some reason. Whenever this happens, and it seems to do so more often in vicious currents, don't move or change anything. Repeat the cast a couple of times. Surely this is possible if you have not moved your feet or changed the amount of line off the reel. If that doesn't bring it back, I shorten up by a foot, then 2 feet, then lengthen by 3 feet, then 4, so as to have covered the area where it was when it rose 2 feet on either side. They are still there, and this usually works. If you've been working a run of water for a time and it has been quiet, and you have any doubts about the fly in use, you can also change flies—providing you don't lose the spot that marks its lie.

This system of working an inlet can take longer if you are interrupted by an occasional take. On runs that are long enough to keep you occupied for a period, often so much time has been consumed that the bass have taken up more positions in water already fished. If I have been fishing a while, I just start working the run all over again. Most nights, in better outflows, I will farm the spot in those parallel arcs twice or more. Plus, because the water has been running longer later, I frequently actually hook up on more stripers on the second pass. Even on a bad night, there has to be something holding there waiting for a bauble of bait. Of course what helps is to have been there enough times to have confidence in the spot, the pattern choice, and the method you employ. What can I say about experience that has not already been said by every philosopher since Plato?

Many openings are surprisingly shallow, and you can draw fish to the top of the water column with only a floating line. Often fish will be on the move, and these tend to be a little higher so that they will take from a higher-drifted offer. Recall that they have to have water running through their gills, and even the linesides going out, while dropping down, are doing so backward and looking up into the current. Also, the edge of the current is popular with them so that when your fly ends its swing, you could get a wrap. I would say that as long as the water is not over 6 feet deep, a floating line will cover most situations.

People often ask what tide is the most productive because they assume that surfcasting is a magical secret that, once learned, becomes the keys to the castle. I have always said that there is no best tide because the question has to be presented connected to a place and its conditions. Tide is—and I talk about this elsewhere in this book—just one of the many characters in the play about conditions. Further, there is another valuable consideration in the study of inlets that begs attention here—water volume.

WATER VOLUME

Chatham Inlet on Cape Cod, which incidentally is one of the most productive inlets in my repertoire, is about 2 miles wide at its opening with the Atlantic. Thus, any bass that might visit Pleasant Bay could pass anywhere at that opening at high tide when the water is 10 feet deep. Nevertheless, at low tide 98 percent of the opening is shoal water, sandy, and only inches deep, even exposed in some places during spring tides. Therefore, at low tide the channel on the south edge of the opening is the only water deep enough for stripers to exit Pleasant Bay. Now I fish a run of water that is forced, because of the reduced volume of water, down to 2 percent of the opening that allowed them in. They have to come by those who fish for them. This explains why Chatham Inlet regulars, though I doubt they know why, love to fish there the last two hours of the drop past slack low, which is later because of lag. A similar situation exists at the Pamet River in Truro, and I have seen this many times on the Maine coast. Just remember that the volume issue is more dynamic in places where there is the greater exchange of water. Also watch for exceptions to this rule.

INLET CULTS

Martha's Vineyard and Nantucket have any number of great pond openings that are ritualistically opened at different times of the year to provide new water for the marine life there. When they are opened—and it is a ritual mindful of old home week—every able-bodied surfcaster on the island gets there to cash in. Now why would they do that?

The Friday nights of my youth were spent in a local gin mill that was supported by a variety of two-fisted beer-drinking, pickled-egg-eating, poker-playing sportsmen who, in addition to women, talked about one thing—fishing. My friend the late Johnny Koback, when he wasn't arm wrestling for a beer, lived and breathed striped bass. Holding court one wintry night, snow drifting against the wheels of our redneck pickups, he desperately sought to explain the basics of shore fishing for the wily striper.

Dragging his finger through the foam of his glass, he would impatiently draw a wet circle on the bar, an opening in that circle, and a channel that led to the sea.

"The tide goes down, the water goes out and draws the bass in. The bass get in the current to eat. The surfcaster throws in the current and gets the bass. What could be easier to understand than that?"

Banging his hand on the bar, he would bellow, "Bartender, give these wet-behind-the-ears kids a drink."

Fly-Fishing Water in Order of Importance

1. Inlets

2. Bays

3. Flats

4. Beaches

5. Rocky shores

4

Conditions

The Nitty-Gritty of Surfcasting

It is natural for people to want to simplify their understanding of fly fishing the striper surf and the behavior of striped bass. Everyone wants an uncomplicated formula to apply that will lead to the rich rewards that have made all surfcasting famous. Were it that simple, of course, we would all grasp what conditions were magic and, as a result, no stripers would remain. In fact, it is complicated because the list of conditions that dictate bass movement and behavior is as long as your arm. Moreover, to keep this formula from being too easy, the conditions, and how they relate to and influence one another, change everything. For instance, it is not enough to know that an onshore wind contributes to the fishing. If it is February the bass are a thousand miles away in warmer water, which serves to illustrate the relationship between wind and temperature.

Cover: Darkness

Most of the predators on our planet are nocturnal and some, because they are another creature's solution, rely upon darkness for protection as well. For us humans, there is something counterintuitive about

Warning: If you are afraid of the dark, buy a boat and some sunscreen.

fishing and moving about in the night—a situation for which we are poorly equipped. It is therefore necessary for us to stop thinking of the world in the way we "see" it and try to understand that the animals in the world function differently.

Fishing from shore is replete with disadvantages. Among them is that most gamefish, unless they have been presented with feeding opportunities that overcome their survival instincts, will not risk the shallows inherent to shorelines until they are provided with cover. This comes in three forms: depth, rough water, and darkness. Depth and rough water are now-and-then elements. Darkness is the only factor that presents itself dependably, and is the one most reliable for both fisher and fish. Therefore, it is incumbent upon surfcasters to plan most, if not all, of their fishing around the night. This is why you will see reference to the word *night* repeatedly throughout this book.

FISH AND LIGHT—WHO SEES WHAT?

The trap in how fishermen think is that they are fundamentally tied to how man views the world. What we all forget is that other animals are equipped with senses that work very differently. This is why some animals function best during the day while others are nocturnal. Maybe if we all understood better how fish see and the influence of light upon their behavior, we would be better equipped to go after them. The first order is to understand that fish—like many mammals—see better than we do in what we call darkness. While the vision of all animals functions similarly, some of us have a distribution of rods and cones that allows us to enjoy better vision in the daytime while others see better in darkness and still others, like fish, adapt daily to the variations in available light. Deer see best in darkness, man sees better in light, and fish—which we had best do here—work well with both. However, that is not a scientific study in visual acumen. Rather, it is an examination of the behavior triggered by different light conditions, natural and otherwise.

All fish see well in the dark. I don't know if it is useful to guess how much better they see than we do, but I have fished at night since I was old enough to go out the back door alone, over sixty years. I fished for bullheads at night when they just would not bite in the day. I also popped and glugged jitterbugs and surface crawlers all night long for largemouths. I laugh when people talk about brown trout being nocturnal when *all* trout feed at night. Back when I fished for Atlantic salmon, I used to toss and turn until I went down to the river in the middle of the night to shake the angling DTs and actually caught more salmon than I did during the day. My most memorable lesson in the value of night fishing came in the striper surf on Charlestown Breachway one midsummer when every light source in our universe was on the other side of the planet. There was a new moon, fog, cloud cover, and no outside light sources. A nun's closet, you could not see your hand in front of your own face. Water was dropping between the jetties and there was a good sea running, so even if there had been any light it still had to penetrate a carpet of thick foam. When my deep-running jig—really no bigger than an average striper fly—swung through them, they took. I never questioned a striper's ability to function in "darkness" after that.

Only rarely is it truly full dark for those fishing. If you have adjusted to the reduced light, you can do just about anything but change flies without a light. What can alter your vision is an artificial light, which will also send gamefish hell west and crooked. Harder to measure is the influence of sunlight during the day upon a person who has not worn sunglasses.

You also have to know what to look for and how it will appear under the light conditions with which you are dealing. Often, depending upon the height of surf, you will know where to look by the sounds that gamefish make while slurping and slopping. Breaking fish will appear as dark stains on the water. The bait they are feeding on will influence their behavior to the extent that some small bass will make big splashes when incited by, say, mackerel or mullet. Big bass might sip little critters like shrimp or sand eels so lightly that you think they are mere schoolies. I have also seen them punishing hickory shad in the first wave; it looked like someone was throwing hand grenades in the surf.

MOON AND LUMINOSITY

Ours is a culture of moon worshipers, and theories abound about which phase inspires the greatest activity in gamefish. There is no simple answer. The subject is fraught with junk science, which mixes the variables. There are twelve stages of luminosity and four basic moon phases. Full is the brightest phase and new the darkest, both of which generate greater tides. As a result, many fishers, who enjoy robust tide rips during a moon tide, attribute results to the light or lack of it when it is more a case of moving water appealing to the fish. Then there are the theories of gravitational pull upon the water, brain fluids in fish as well as fisher, animal behavior, and excitation—so if you hear *Twilight Zone* music in the background, I hear it, too.

Much of what is believed about moon phase relates to culture rather than anything else. For instance, when I fished with New Yorkers in P-town, they all swore that the best fishing there was on a full moon. The smart ones, also from New York, came two weeks later when there was nobody around. Success was equal per man for both groups, but being first all the time on a red-hot rip because you were alone gave total darkness an edge. For me, better fishing usually came when the light changed.

Over and over we used to have the fish timed with a level of tide. Then we began noticing that gamefish didn't take until the moon rose to our eastern horizon. Similarly, we always counted upon Race Bar on the Outer Cape to give up some good fishing at low tide. Yet one week per month we would be getting bass like crazy with the moon setting on the western horizon; it would end once the moon set and its resultant darkness occurred. We attributed it to the change in light. If there is one moon phase that I do not like it is the full when it occurs on a clear night; you can actually fish as though it were day. These are wild animals that rely upon darkness for cover, and I believe they are reluctant to risk the shallows without that cover.

Everything in the natural world plays musical chairs at the daily change in light of dawn and dusk. Rods and cones are being adjusted for that timing, and the new situation seems to excite wildlife, fish no exception. I'm not sure that I can adequately explain the reason, but the dawn gives up way better fishing than sunset. The flaw in dawn fishing is that it ends with full light whereas evenings you will often find gamefish at sunset and then be able to extend the opportunity well on into the night. Darkness for shore fishers is the time. It is for boat fishing as well, but boat fishing is so much better all the way around that boaters don't have to put up with the inconvenience of fumbling around in the dark. For surfcasters night fishing is so important that you will learn to dislike June 21 because of the short seven hours of darkness. Some fly fishers lament fishing in darkness, but if you have any experience at all from a day fishing background, night moves quickly progress to second nature. Certainly, if you have been fly casting all your life, it is not challenging to do so in the dark.

Don't scare them. It is natural for some folks to both distrust and fear the darkness, shining lights all over, flashing the foreshore, and sending fish hell west in terror. Whether you're in fresh or salt, nothing will end fishing faster. The obvious reason for this is that the flash of a light is usually sudden, which will startle any predator. Also, an abrupt, as opposed to gradual, change in light creates light shock, which is similar to coming out of a movie theater into sunlight. If you are into fish and a vehicle comes down the beach, indiscreet use of headlights can shut things down for up to twenty minutes. Of course the bass or blues usually come right back, probably once their eyes have adjusted. Some surfcasters go to great pains to be cautious about this, but you still don't want to hit anything, anybody, or, worse, drive into the water doing it.

People who smoke should not light up facing the water. When changing flies, turn your back to the fishing or even move away from the location. You cannot be too careful. When you cast moving shadows on the water by walking between any light source—natural or otherwise—and the sea, you are spooking the fish by projecting the movement of shadows onto them.

Nature has done a marvelous job of equipping wild animals with the camo needed to survive the predatory world in which they live. Salmonids have a unique coloration that includes enough dots to simulate stones and gravel found on a stream's bottom. Largemouth bass carry the green they need, and smallmouths sport enough brown to simulate the sunken leaves found in a rocky stream bottom. Stripers, with dusky hues and form-breaking lines, do not stand out; and green bluefish hide well in the colors that have been given to them. Still, nature has failed them all in one way—no matter how they seem to blend into their environment, they all cast a shadow, which gives them away. Indeed, it is possible to walk the banks of a river and find gamefish holding in the current—fresh or salt—because their bodies block off enough light for them to have a shadow. A fish might be well hidden, but not its shadow.

In daylight, penetration of the surface glare of fishing waters is basic to seeing what is below. If your view penetrates the depths, you will see obstructions, structure, and fish slicks, all of which are clear evidence of roaming gamefish and—most important—the fish themselves, which will sometimes follow your fly. Seeing into the water is accomplished by wearing Polaroids, not ordinary sunglasses. A simple test to determine whether glasses are equipped with the polarizing quality is to turn known Polaroids at 90 degrees to the pair in doubt. If both are suitable, they will block out all light and the lenses will appear to be black. Sight fishing is just that, and it begins with wearing the proper glasses. Certainly no one who walks the banks of a stream doing a visual search can do so without the help of glasses. Even beach fishers who do all their angling after dark, as they should, will be in sunlight going off at daybreak or coming on at nightfall. If I had a quarter for every time we saw a large bass or a pod of bait that led us to cow bass, the jar would be full. Shadows are a product of the light conditions and belong in this discussion.

Back when we lived on the beach, we fished every night with four kids. Fishing until they went off to college, our twin daughters, Susan and Sandra, one season discovered a condition on the east-facing Outer Cape that was so rare that I don't know if I could ever hope to see it repeated. It was at the time of the month when the moon was sagging lower in the western sky at enough of an angle to project a shadow of a high dune on the sea in North Truro. The girls, who had a way of doing things that was clear to each other but no one else, would go down the beach away from our vehicle, cast into the lighted portion of the surf, permitting their plugs to swing under tension into the shadow of the dune. When their plugs swung into the shadow, they would hook up as the linesides apparently lay in wait for what was coming. Admonishing them for not fishing closer to the buggy, I could not get them to come nearer to us. Finally, in frustration, I walked higher along the dune and could see them shoulder to shoulder whispering in the way that conspirators—especially twin conspirators—can do when they don't want you to know something. Yet the situation would only repeat on the following night. And when the tide was the same two weeks later, the moon was at the same angle in the eastern sky that gave no shadow. You had to wait a month to do it, and a cloud cover could kill it. Around the same time, and that was twenty-five years ago, though I see no reason why that would change, we used to make a point of fishing Race Point Light in P-town. Then they allowed campers there, and people used to park huge walk-ins at the top of the beach where the vehicle's shadow was projected every thirteen seconds on the water each time the Race Light made a revolution. Our little girls, the little buggers, had by chance discovered that if they cast a couple of seconds before the light's rotation in a lighted section of surf uptide of a buggy, letting it swing under tension into the vehicle's dark shadow, a lineside would smash their plugs. It had gotten so dependable for them that I found them quarreling over the use of a particular well-placed rig and its shadow, which drew from a good section of the Race rip. Having dibs over a particular shadow had two compensations: good fishing and the chance to outdo their parents—something they only rarely missed. By the time I had sufficient room for a backcast the shadows were behind me, so I could never make it work at the top of the tide with flies. At low tide, however, with conditions equal, the fly was always better than any Rebel could be.

PHOSPHORESCENCE (FIRE)

Swarms of microorganisms—called dinoflaggellates by scientists—will glow when tipped by the water movement, passing bait, or gamefish. There are hundreds of species of phosphorescent plankton in the oceans of the world, and books say that they can be as numerous as five hundred to the inch. On very dark nights the phosphorescent plankton, what regulars call "fire," is accentuated by the absence of light. Darkness doesn't produce the fire condition, but it is more evident in the absence of light. Fly lines tip up more fire than small-diameter mono, but fly fishers will still do well with slow retrieves. Also, the smallness of the fly, when compared to the average plug, is an advantage when dealing with spooky gamefish that are edgy because of the fire. During bright nights the fire will likely not show. Or it will appear with the setting of the moon; conversely, it will subside at moonrise. It can be a curse when every slight motion in your line is both magnified and accentuated.

These bioluminescent organisms—which are not pollution—can be very spooky, and even your own fly can startle you into thinking that you are being attacked by something yet undiscovered by the scientific community. While fire is not unusual, it is just one more circumstance to add to the list of conditions to consider so that you are kept from determining why fishing is good or bad.

There is little to be said about fire; it is just one more item to deal with. I don't know if bass follow our flies more in fire, or if the fire exposes this ornery and offensive habit that we might not otherwise know about, but they do follow. I have stood in the stuff with bass and bluefish zinging through the bait—it is quite a show. The bait is a school of sparks running from a spark machine with the illuminated whoosh of a striper or blue lunging at them within seconds. The blues have a faster scoot. A pipsqueak 20-inch bass can look big enough to hurt you, and an outsized striper can be downright frightening.

Fishing in this material succeeds with fewer casts, smaller flies, and slower retrieves. The idea is to bump and upset as few of these sparkly little glow bugs as possible. The fire's visible intensity is inversely proportional to light. Depending upon the intensity of the plankton bloom, a full or quarter moon is usually enough to allay the condition. The wise surfcaster keeps moon phase in mind, realizing that you are either going to lose your light with moon set or gain light with a rise in the moon that puts the fire out. If you have fish and fire is ruining your chances, it could get mighty good after the moon rises—a classic example of conditions and their change.

LIGHTHOUSES

Most lighthouses are placed at strategic locations that match up with a prominent point or sea opening. You have to wonder if the people who decide where lighthouses go are the same ones deciding where they are going to fish. Because the light is constant, almost natural in a way, the passing of the light does not negatively impact stripers or fishing for them. In fact, and we have seen this at the Cape's Highland and Race Point Lights, as well as Rhody's Point Judith Light, that sudden but rhythmic burst of light puts the fire out long enough for a follower to take. All the better if there is fog, because the droplets of water suspended in the air bounce the light around in a dull gray glow, easily doubling the effect of the rotating light. Plankton dislike lumens.

Cover: Rough-Water Surf

Even surf fishers with only a cursory level of experience do not like a calm flat day at the shore. Most know enough not to expect much action until dark. Still, when the water is kicked up with a windswept

Rough water provides cover for stripers, and while your cast is shorter, the fish are closer. As the song goes, "Know when to fold."

surf—waves, foam—it is possible to find some action in the day. I would not put this condition at the top of my list, but if I had action the night before, and had good water, it would be worth a try. The thing is that this kind of water is not usually fishable with the fly rod. Nevertheless, a compensating notion is that bass could be so close that in spite of an onshore gale, you might be able to reach them. It would depend upon your ability to deal with wind and whether that wind was quartering enough to keep the fly away from your ear. A rough sliding surf can make the management of stripping impossible without a stripping basket. When it is not behind you, your fly line, even if it floats, could end up around both legs, adding a coil this way and that without effective line management.

Keep in mind that you can stack these cover-providing conditions where you would benefit from both rough water and darkness. Of course I have seen rough-water stripers during the day chasing summer squid. For them, it was like a party. However, the time I'm talking about we did not fly fish because we could not have.

GENTLE SURF

Some open beaches are famous for their gentle—to no—surf. Places like these are the product of their placement, prevalent winds, and protection. Consequently, it is possible to fish the open sea without a wave to upset your stripping. Island backsides, as with some shores of Martha's Vineyard, Nantucket, or Block Island, provide this kind of fishing. My best experience with this fly-fishing boon is Cape Cod from High Head back northwest around the Cape's horn south to Long Point. You will of course find this flat, waveless water inside Long Island Sound clear, wind depending, east to Buzzards Bay. When fishing this kind of water, your stripping is not being swept about, and it is very easy to identify striper activity on the darkest night.

The best fly fishing for bass is in flat water.

Cover: Depth

The depth needed to put striped bass off their guard is not usually available to surfcasters. I recall one of those memorable blitzes in Provincetown in the 1970s at the Traps, just east of Race Light, which drop off very quickly. We had them on a Saturday night at sunset among a spread of plug fishers. The following night, wind from behind and most people having gone home so that there were only a handful of us, I actually caught more on an eel fly with a fast-sinking line than the others with their traditional Atom plugs. What hurt my score, and these were all big fish of 20 to 35 pounds, was that I could not bring them in as fast as those with casting rods.

The jetties that flank inlets in Rhode Island provide deep enough water for day fishing. You just have to use a sinking line and pick your spots carefully. Yet I emphasize that, in my opinion, day fishing is borderline stunt fishing for surfcasters.

DAYLIGHT

Against the backdrop of how I feel it is safe for me to address what day fishing you might experience, as long as you understand that these are exceptions. I have been in on numerous blitzes where we took fish in the day. Most, however, were extensions of night fishing when the sun came up and maybe the wind was kicking up the surf or the bass stormed the beach at sunset. Most of the day fishing we have had was at either end of the day. The biggest bass I ever caught (see chapter 5, "Situations That Teach") was from an extended night blitz that lasted into the dawn. Other than those two occasions, I don't remember even trying to fly fish in the day. It has become unnatural for me.

Fall-migration fishing provides nearly unfair examples of possible day fishing because when the bass are on the move, they are crazy, opportunistic, wildly competitive, and will usually take anything. Even then, such behavior is more likely exhibited at night.

Tide

Questions relating to the best tide for fishing are legion. People cannot get over the notion there is a magic tide that provides the best fishing. In reality, you cannot answer questions that relate to tide unless it is regarding a specific location. There are many locations that do have a best tide, and regulars who fish these places often know it. When fish tend to exhibit leanings for a certain tide at a specific place, the issue of a particular tide begins to take on meaning. At many locations tide is not a factor at all in the productivity of the fishing. Along some long stretches of beach where the movement of water is not impeded, or in areas of the coast where the tidal exchange is slight, the tide is of little consequence. Generally, the surfcaster's quest for moving water is more easily satisfied by moving north from the equator. In New England we see dramatic differences in tidal exchange among Rhode Island with a 4-foot extreme, Cape Cod's 11-foot difference, then on to the Maritimes, where it is over 20 feet. However, a locale is not better fishing because it has greater tides. There are too many other considerations that influence the fishing for any generalization to be suitable. Still, anytime you see a correlation between good fishing and a particular tide, you should make note of it so as to cash in on it regularly. Often these are not secrets.

Were you to ask me to name a place for a specific tide, I am certain that I could name one for low, high, incoming, dropping, slack low, and slack high. This of course can be refined so that an area with its mix of hot spots could provide reliable fishing for any hour of the night. Experienced surfcasters, and fly fishermen on the shore are surfcasters, commonly draw upon a refined repertoire of known tide-dependent locations from which they can fish. They even know when to move.

As you accumulate information that makes you more tide-wise, it is helpful to keep a log that pins down what you have learned. Invariably, that log will contain a lot of worthless, even erroneous observations about some places. You have no way of knowing that until later.

MOON AND TIDE

Most people know that the moon influences tide but lack understanding of the purity in its cycle. When the moon is "full," or large and round in the night sky, and when it is "new" or large and round in the day and very dark at night, we experience the greatest exchange of water, what are called spring tides, although they have nothing to do with the seasons. These tides also generate extremes in available light—bright and dark. Tides will occur at the same time according to moon phase within minutes. For instance, with a full or new moon in

Boston, the area from, say, Cape Cod to Portland, Maine, will always have a high tide around midnight. The tide will also move up around fifty minutes per twenty-four-hour period so that a week later the hour that offered high tide will offer low. We usually round it off to an hour per night so that it is possible to predict the tide based upon the particular known phase of the moon. Tide charts are fine and I have no problem with them. But they serve people who, because of domestic and professional commitments, are not fishing every night.

In our study of conditions here, knowing the moon phase we are fishing tells us what the light is likely to be—a classic example of the interrelationship of conditions. It gets telling when the moon rises in the middle of the night with a kind of subdued light that comes from a last quarter or sets at the same hour two weeks later, exhibiting phosphorescence the casters did not even know was there. All tied together, aren't they?

Do I get mail? People are always asking me when they should go fishing. Not that I always know, but they commonly exhibit a lack of understanding of the conditional concoction. For instance, they want to go to a spot that is famously productive at low tide. They know that it should be dark when they fish this low-tide hot spot. So they plan their trip around a full or new moon for its robust tidal exchange, which always—for the next million years—has a high tide at midnight. Consequently their low tides occur in daylight. Duh!

The understanding of conditions and the way they relate to one another points up the many trade-offs the student of conditions must be willing to make. If you want low tide in the deep night in Boston, you have to be willing to accept neap tides—the ones with less exchange of water. If you despise fire in the water, then you must know when the moon will set or when it will rise. Learn to eat your lunch after the moon is set, or sleep in the evening and go surfcasting when the moon comes up. It can all be predicted.

One last example because I'm getting tired of preaching about all of this. Some spots are always good, but I cannot reach them until the tide goes out. I fish a section of Race Point where I can reach the bass for only a few minutes while the Race rip is forming in the early part of the rise. As the tide comes up I am driven farther inland, away from the fish that are still lying exactly where they were an hour earlier. I have reached them with a shooting head on calm nights, but usually end up going over my waders trying to stay with them.

Wind

I have purposely revealed much that can be said about wind in other sections here because wind commonly has a relationship with other conditions. Isolating wind in the conditions mix may lead students of environmental factors in the wrong direction. Providing that wind can be dealt with adequately by anglers, it usually provides cover in the form of rough seas while creating some vulnerability in baitfish. Often—but there are still other considerations—stripers are closer to the beach in an onshore wind. However, how much fly fishing is available in an onshore is a combination of angling skill and wind intensity, and only you can decide how far you want to take the effort. It is always a good idea to have other tackle options when the wind overwhelms the fly-fishing surfcaster.

Many places are dramatically enhanced by wind from certain quarters, and knowing which direction for a particular location can be a predictor for blitz fishing. An example that points up the symbiotic relationship between wind and tide is Race Point on the Cape, where the southwest helps the dropping tide. In contrast, a northeast wind helps the rise in tide. In these examples wind helps tide rips pump harder when both share the same direction. A caster who is acquainted with a particular rip will see the difference during the first cast and swing. Moreover, the fishing is better.

Weather

The only aspect of weather that seems to influence fish behavior and our ability to fish is wind. The other factors that spring from intense weather only play into fishing if they prevent anglers from functioning. Certainly, if it is too cold, angling methods have to be modified to accommodate temperatures. I find that I cannot fly fish below 18 degrees, and if there is additional windchill, that element has to be taken into account. Even late season, the best fly fishing is at night, and those temperatures commonly are upon us in November and December. You see a lot of bait fishing on the beaches at this time for that reason. I have fished conventionally in whiteout snow, but I have only fly fished in snowfall for trout and steelhead.

Rain is not an issue in fish behavior, except that the cloud cover accompanying it might enhance what little day fishing takes place.

All fishing is condition dependent, and the striper surf is no exception.

Certainly a cloud cover might tone down moonlight during a full moon or when the quarters are in evidence and actually help the fishing. Bright nights are not good.

Some of the most wildly blitz surf fishing I have ever experienced took place both before a passing hurricane and after. Still, it is necessary to remind you that people are commonly killed on the coast by hurricanes, to say nothing of losing a car or buggy from violent surf. Also, water that is turned up by a storm is overwhelmed with suspended silt and weed for half a mile or more from shore. For each hurricane that has ever yielded good fishing, there have been a hundred that ruined it. Keep this in mind when you make travel plans for fishing and be ready to cancel.

Water Temperature

People are always trying to explain the reason for bad fishing, and a common way to go about it is to say that the water is too warm. I have never been able to determine what the point of water temperature might be where stripers sulk inactively because I doubt that it has been demystified. I know that for the many years when I fished on Cape Cod I was acquainted with surfcasters from New Jersey and Long Island, and they often found the Cape fishing with its 55-degree water in July to be less productive than it was where they came from. The water at home for them had to be above the 71 degrees that I measured on July 29, 1967, when I caught a 51-pounder in Rhode Islander. Nor was this a behavioral anomaly; I was acquainted with a number of boatmen catching stripers even larger than this during other seasons in that tepid water temperature. And as I write this in the summer of 2003, our best yield of postmoratorium 50-pound stripers is being experienced between Montauk and Cuttyhunk at water that is above 70 degrees F. I can safely say that the low 70s are not a problem. Similarly, bass are commonly caught in the mid- and low 50s water temperatures from Cape Cod north.

A recurrent spring-arrival bellwether for small bass, usually, but not necessarily in April west of Monomoy, where the water is warmer—South Cape Beach, Rhode Island, and Connecticut—is 50 degrees. We have no way of determining if the season's start is triggered by migration tied to that temperature or if the fish are there but not feeding until the temperature is reached. And while we can predict striper arrivals with water temperature, less seems to be known about departure and its relationship with water temperature. The reason for this apparently relates to a plethora of influences—tired fishers, cold air temperatures, social pressures, hunting season, even Christmas shopping. I do know that bass are caught from New England beaches way past the time when traditional fishing ends, and I have come home from a hunting trip on snow and caught a mix of bluefish in with my stripers. Generally, blues indicate that more time is available to striper fish—it is assumed that blues leave first, as they seem less tolerant of the cold.

Stripers behave differently in warm water than in cold. The first thing you notice—if you have been catching bass in cold water—is that they do not fight as well in 70-degree temperatures. We had frequent opportunity to make this comparison when we fished on the Cape in July and then went to Rhode Island for August. They do not survive release as well. This could relate to the buildup of lactic acid being greater in a warm-water environment when under the stress of fighting.

Water temperatures respond slowly to the air's influence at both ends of the season. It takes a long time for the Atlantic to catch up with the air in spring. Similarly, in fall the water is able to resist cooling influences. If the autumn cooling is moderate, the unfavorable cool-down of water is delayed. The water's mass does not respond quickly to air temperature. Rather, it takes a prolonged period of cold to exert enough influence to draw down the temperature. The lag, the difference, between air and water temperatures, which is at least a month, can have you casting into 60-degree water with the air in the 30s—the seas steaming from the resistance to change.

Early-season water only has to climb about 12 degrees in New England from its low point. Autumn water, on the other hand, has to descend more than 20 degrees, adding to the time of departure and making it less predictable.

Pollution

Like you, I am never fond of seeing the waters of the Striper Coast fouled with pollution, although the striped bass has exhibited a keen tolerance for both chemical and organic pollution. Both the Chesapeake and Hudson provide a dangerous mixture of pesticide runoff, acid rain, and PCBs. Yet none of the contaminants seems to have had any deleterious effect upon the linesides, either reproductively or otherwise. Indeed, polluted harbors and rivers seem to do little to repel them. In late spring of 2003 there was so much rain runoff that the city of Providence had to cease treating its storm drains and permit the flow of raw sewage into Narragansett Bay, a perennial problem. The water was so murky that my wife and I could not see our wader-clad feet, but the fishing was memorable nonetheless.

New Haven Harbor is not exactly a pristine tourist attraction. Nevertheless, in 1992 Steve Franco landed a 75-pound, 6-ounce striper less than 100 feet from shore. He was not fly fishing, but his is an example of the kind of bass that are not discouraged by what would seem to us to be intolerable water conditions.

These environmental factors and their interrelationships only tell us where fishing is good. However, to find good fishing yourself, you must know why it is good. Even so the striper surf holds its mysteries. Anytime I find stripers in a place with any regularity, I find myself wondering what little unseen condition made it happen.

Conditions That Count, in Order of Importance

1. Darkness and light
2. Tide
3. Wind—intensity and direction
4. Gentle surf
5. Rough water
6. Depth
7. Phosphorescence
8. Weather
9. Water temperature
10. Pollution

5

Situations That Teach

A recurrent theme with which you will be confronted here is the effectiveness of fly fishing when compared to other methods—say, lure casting or bait fishing. I do not advocate fly fishing for its own sake. Rather, it should only be chosen because it is a superior way to catch striped bass in the surf. I am going to share with you an experience our son, Dick, and I had thirty-five years ago that addresses fly fishing's superiority and teaches some important lessons at the same time.

A Popular Striper Surf Standard

In the early 1960s Laurie Rapala's Finnish balsa-wood minnow creations stormed the world of sportfishing. Fishing with them, casters took pike, redfish, weakfish, bluefish, and striped bass, to name only some of the species. Rapala's success inspired an entire genre of plugs that set the stage for numerous knockoffs—Rebels, Red-Fins, Bombers, Mambos—all minnows that resembled the original and were at their best in floater models. In a few short years, a following sprang up on the Striper Coast devoted entirely to fishing Rebels for striped bass. Curiously, different and diverse groups of anglers, who had little or no contact with each other, learned the same thing: The best way to surfcast for stripers is to tie a Rebel direct and fish the beach with it at night. This simple revelation became the standard by which all other angling choices could be judged.

Fly Fishing Emerges for Us

In 1970 we were involved in a situation at Race Point in Provincetown on Cape Cod where we were catching dozens of school bass that averaged between 6 and 10 pounds. Each night, and we were rod-and-reel commercials then, we cast into the teeth of a sou'west gale with plugs equipped with eel fly teasers. When the wind became too strong for plugs, we resorted to using bank sinkers as casting weights. (This *is* a fly-fishing story, so stay with me on this.) Then the wind calmed.

On a quiet night I broke out the fly rod, using the same eel fly pattern that had done so well as a teaser and also when cast with a sinker. I was not surprised to clean up with the pattern, as it seemed to me that it was better than any of the other choices for which I had opted when the wind was up. Meanwhile our son, Dick, who was twelve at the time, fished with light spinning gear using a ½-ounce, 5½-inch floater Rebel. Unplanned, Dick was the control for the fly-fishing experiment. Well, if you want to see a glum, sad little surfcaster, that was Dick when his father outfished him three to one with the fly. The following night, however, he came out with his own fly rod and redeemed himself. For us the evidence was beginning to point to the superiority of the fly—as long as the wind was not pumping out at 50 knots, a common occurrence at Race Point.

Then our buddy Roger, an accomplished surfcaster, came out for the weekend with his spinning rod, and we told him how good the fishing was and encouraged him to come with us. There was no point in making an issue of fly fishing because, as with so many traditional surfcasters, in his mind fly fishing was something that was done by those interested in trout. It has always been, still is, viewed with disdain as a sort of stunt-fishing gimmickry in the esoteric hard-core world of surfcasters to which we belong.

That night Roger showed up with all his spinning tackle on the roof of his buggy, along with at least one pool-cue conventional intended for monster fishing—choices in which I have also always engaged. Dick and I proceeded to hook and land one lineside after another, each of us landing three to his one. I did not like doing this to Roger, but even if we'd had another fly rod, he would not have known what to do with it.

The following night Roger showed up with a teaser rigged ahead of his plug, using a 7-inch Rebel as a casting weight. Resorting to a teaser fly ahead of a plug is a universal solution to folks confronted with exceptional fly fishing for the first time. They never seem to understand that there is a difference. This raised his score up slightly from the night before, perhaps four to our ten. Then he tried a smaller

We found that fly fishing was much more productive than proven striper surf standards of success. 1970 photo.

Rebel, hoping that the bass would also take the plug because the few he was getting were all on the fly—the teaser fly, not a fly-fished fly. What also hurt him was that he spent much of the night rummaging through hundreds of dollars' of tackle, looking for a secret formula that could hose down his embarrassment. You can't catch fish with a flashlight in your mouth while frantically throwing plugs all over the inside of your beach buggy. There is a lesson from this story. It is that when measured against the basis by which all surfcasting is judged, the method employed by dyed-in-the-wool spin fishers, Rebels in the deep night, fell so far short of our fly-fishing technique that I would never question the value of fly fishing in the striper surf. It yields three fish for every one you would catch with the next best option.

Beside the Best Surfcasters

On the Cape I was intimate with a New York surfcaster whom I wish I could name because he is well known for being a highliner with rigged eels. Rigged eels are poison on stripers, particularly big ones, and one of my largest, 52 pounds, was taken that way. The person will be left unnamed because I don't want to taint examples intended to teach by damaging anyone's angling reputation, especially someone so competent. During the same period in the deep night, around the same time, I pulled up at Race Bar at the right stage of tide just as he was arriving from his rigged-eel fishing on the Back Beach. We walked down to the water together to a hard-swinging, left-to-right rip. Each time the Race Light made its rotation, sand eels would sprinkle in my fore. At least half the time that the light illuminated my foreground—and it cycled every thirteen seconds—I could see the dark forms of bass swirling only a few yards out. I hooked up as soon as I was able to strip enough line off the reel. The other guy's eel hit the water and he began his rhythmic pumping. Not wanting him to see me, I worked my bass left and tried to move it up to my buggy between rotations of the lighthouse. You can't do much in thirteen seconds. In the time I was gone, however, he never hooked a fish. I am certain that he was seeing what I was doing, and I also know, because I knew just about everybody who could make a surf rod sing, that not an awful lot could happen around him that would evade him.

Next cast, I hooked roughly a 15-pounder, which was a little better striper than I had been catching and certainly big enough to inhale a rigged eel. Anyway, because I don't want to take too long with this, because I know you get the point, I beached half a dozen mediums while he failed entirely to connect before the tide slacked there and the fish moved on.

Because I knew that I was not fooling anyone, and he was a perfect gentleman anyway, never crowding me, my fish were piled in a small heap near where I was fishing. Walking over to examine the pile, he said, "I wouldn't a believed it if I didn't see it with me own eyes! And with a trout rod."

It was not just the compliment. It was the source.

Most Surfcasters Reject Fly Fishing

In those days—late 1960s and early '70s—there were hundreds of serious surf fishers on Cape Cod. We lived among them, knew all the regulars. Do you know how many people were engaged in fly fishing the beaches of the Outer Cape—Nauset Beach to Long Point? The answer is none. Let me give you one more example, and I'll let you get back to the tying bench and vise.

In 1977, a season when P-town enjoyed the greatest surfcasting blitz it had ever known, it was possible to fish all night and find big stripers in the surf everywhere you went. I saw more 50-pound-plus linesides taken in the surf than I have ever seen anywhere in my life. People were so spoiled by the marvelous fishing that they would not walk 40 feet to look at a 40-pounder. It was the kind of fishing that made you want grandchildren just so you could tell them what surfcasting for stripers used to be.

Our son and I had been fishing a steady pick on the Back Beach with rhino gear—pool-cue rods, squidders casting rigged eels, and Atom plugs bigger than brook trout—when we realized that the tide was down enough to fish Race Point Bar. When we rounded the curve of the beach, a glance told us something was going on because of the gaggle of beach buggies spread out on the low-tide-exposed bar.

"Nobody knows what they are," George Carlezon told me as we slipped in with headlights off.

Three surfcasters in waders were standing at the water's edge remarking over a fin that slid back and forth, disappeared, then reappeared a few yards away.

"Whatever it is," one of them said, "they're spread all along here, singles. Maybe sharks."

Bewildered by the total lack of fishing, I asked, "Anybody think of maybe throwing a striper plug at them?"

"Oh, we've been throwing everything at them all night. Nobody caught nuthin'."

I was convinced that if anybody could find out, it was this bunch, because there had to be five hundred years' surfcasting experience among them—guys like Paulie Heorcher and Carlezon. I won't try to name them all, but it was a veritable Who's Who of Cape Cod surfcasting standing around sucking their thumbs like tourists, acting like they had no clue how to fish for striped bass. What could I lose?

On the roof of my buggy was a 9-foot two-piece glass fly rod that had been cooking in the sun that season for so long, the sections were welded together at the ferrule. It had the biggest Pflueger Medalist made on it—1498. Pulling it down, I walked over to the nearest "shark" and began stripping line from the reel while these experts began trading snide remarks under their breath about what Swede called "a fooking trout pole." (You have to know where I'm going with this.)

With enough line out to throw past the fin, I worked the eel fly first on one side of this mystery and then the other. Nothing. Then the tantalizing fin swished first this way then that, apparently trying to balance itself on its nose in the shallow water. I waited what seemed like too long, then began the retrieve. Nothing. Casting again, I waited for a full minute for the sinking line to settle in what was possibly 3 feet of water, only this time I pushed the rod tip into the water until I felt the bottom, then began a rhythmic strip. The fin disappeared, and only a few seconds later I felt the fly hang up like it was stuck on something, like I had hooked a stump in some inland swamp. I hauled back as hard as I could and everything seemed to stop like I was stuck on the bottom. Then the brute continued feeding as if nothing had happened.

Before long there was a sense of writhing, when I knew whatever the heck it was, I had caught it. Or had it caught me? Then came the run. The 90 feet of fly line was gone in seconds as the reel groaned, backing melting from the spool. Dick and I chased it for fifteen minutes and I could feel both my cranking hand and fighting arm going dead when he ran down the beach, with 200 feet of line out, and gaffed it in the shallows.

It gets better. Retying another fly, I found another tailing bass, apparently grubbing for sand eels in close. Now that I knew what to do, it was easy to cast beyond the feeding lineside, let the line sink, and stuff the rod tip into the water. The sudden stop came the same way and I drove the fly's steel until the cow felt trouble and headed seaward into the Race, the current that created Cape Cod a few million years ago. This time, however, the water of the Race had turned, and there was a lot more current out there. I was deep into my backing

My biggest fly-fishing striper, this 43-pounder was tailing in the surf. 1977 photo.

when the drag started acting balky. Forces were building where it took more strength to start the turn of the reel against the drag than it took to keep it spinning. There were two torques involved—breakaway and running. If the bass stopped, it took a lot of might to get it started; but once going, it spun effortlessly, giving up precious backing. I could not control the drag, and once the fish had the Race working with her, she lunged, causing the reel to spin violently until it gnarled in a backlash, cutting itself at the spool. I had lost what had to be the fly-fishing world record at the time. Worse, I had lost the means to continue fishing because I knew none of the other stuff would work.

As it turned out, the one striper I landed weighed 43 pounds, which would have been the world record, if not disqualified for using a 20-pound tippet. At the time the maximum allowable tippet strength was 15 pound. Twenty pound was not allowed until years later.

I soon bought a new "salmon reel," which was no easy project on a coast where virtually no big-game fly fishing was carried on. The following night, same location, the tide moved up under an hour, I beached eight bass from 28 to 40 pounds while a gallery of surfcasters watched without making a cast. For them, there was no point. While the new fly reel I had bought the day before had a smoother drag that gave me much better command over the fish I fought, comparisons between the two nights, with two different reels and similar-sized stripers, were not complicated, simple to understand.

The Lessons

On the surface there should be no difference in performance between a fly rigged ahead of a casting weight like a plug and a fly fished alone in customary fly-fishing applications. The use of a teaser, sometimes called a dropper, is now a customary part of the lure caster's bag of tricks. I have been doing this myself for forty years and, when done with care under the right circumstances, a fly ahead of a plug on spinning or conventional gear can be very effective. Those who theorize say that the plug stalking the fly evokes some competitive notion in the striper's mind that makes it hit more readily. It is but one more instance of the junk science that flourishes in the striper surf. I say it that way because we have been able to prove over and over that the fly alone actually catches more. If anything, many of us feel that the plug, with its most profound purpose a casting weight, often distracts the bass so that it hits neither.

It is important to imitate what they are feeding on, which is a variation on that timeworn theme, *match the hatch*. Nevertheless, be certain that your observations of what they are feeding on are accurate. For instance, I was in on a blitz once where the surf was polluted with sand eels, causing all the surfcasters there to assume that in this case sand eels were behind the whole thing. As I dragged a moderate striper, say 25 pounds, to my buggy, I noticed that it disgorged a juvenile weakfish about 8 inches long. While I had enjoyed some success while convinced that this was a sand eel blitz, I caught more with a larger plug that best simulated a weakfish—a saltwater variation on the "masked hatch" theme of fly fishing. Cautions should always be cooking in the mind of the observer. Commonly, fishers will confuse sperling with sand eels because of the physical similarities, but their behavior is totally different. Things are often not what they seem, and if you are among gamefish and not catching them, you had best begin thinking about how you might change something.

Often the bait will act differently, in spite of it being a familiar species to the observer. For instance, sand eels, which are amphibious, will sometimes school and swim along a shore in clouds. Other times they will be left high and dry by an ebbing tide where they are panned by the wave action. When this happens, stripers will be so close to the wet sand of shore that a walking surfcaster's boots grinding sand will send them into deep water in terror.

When we found those monsters tailing on Race Point, they were digging sand eels much in the way that they might dig for sea worms (*Nereis* spp.). Often evidence of a certain behavior can be observed from the bass itself. The time I beached all those big bass when nobody else could, every one had abrasions and scratchy wear on its chin caused by digging. Had folks been observant enough, they might have surmised that the fish were feeding on the bottom and fished accordingly.

When stripers are swimming wildly in a feeding frenzy, they are less likely to display selectivity. In that situation the fly moving along is targeted quickly. However, in deep runs, or beaches where the water drops off quickly, I would always opt to fish a sinking line. Certainly the bottom is the best place to start. When an angler is fishing an extra-fast-sinking line, it is possible to work the deep water effectively as long as the line is not running at 10 feet and the fly at 3. Harmony in sink rate is desirable and attainable by utilizing a shorter leader so as to get the fly at the same height in the water column. Concerns about leader-shy gamefish usually are not valid, and there are no other choices unless you want to wait all night for the fly to catch up with the line.

There are traps in our observations both about identifying the bait upon which stripers are foraging and even about the bass themselves. In the incident above when Race Bar was being dug for sand eels by the moby linesides of the time, there was no excuse for regular, dyed-in-the-wool Cape Cod surfcasters to fail to identify what was in their fore. Indeed, it is rare that it might be anything else but striped bass or bluefish. Still, the notion that they were "sharks" was no doubt inspired by *Jaws*-type movies where the sickle penetrating the surface could only be a shark. In fact, we were all looking at top angles of the bass tail as it struggled to maintain its equilibrium in water less than the bass's length. Even the time when a disgorged weakfish showed plain evidence of their presence, one surfcaster called out that they were driving coho salmon onto the beach. Keep in mind that in addition to the masked hatch situation mentioned above, it is possible to have more than one type of forage. For example, Rhode Island's September mullet run occurs at the same time as when snapper blues are in the waters, and bass eat them both at the same time. I don't begrudge anybody a simple mistake. Quite simply, I seek only to remind you that in a world as complicated as the striper surf, your identification skills—with both bait and gamefish—can enhance your efforts more effectively.

There are more people plug fishing the striper surf than fly fishing, but not because the plugs are better. They do so because it is what they know how to do. The notion of using a fly suffers from being in its infancy, without any solid evidence to the contrary. The Penn squidder benefits from a thirty-year head start on the Pflueger Medalist. Yet when the "traditionalists" were confronted by a situation that—at least at the time—confounded them, they were unaware of the fly-fishing option.

The skilled fly tier should always fashion patterns of different sizes to best imitate the dimensions of the particular bait. Sand eels commonly show up on our beaches anywhere from 2 to 7 inches long. One reason why bucktail is less useful in our patterns is that there are limits to the length of the bucktail, but saddle hackles are longer and can be trimmed down. The first time I confronted the big bass of Race Bar, I already knew that most sand eels were running around 6 inches. I also knew, because of the number of bass we were taking plug and rigged-eel fishing, that I could benefit from as large a hook as I could cast—in this case 3/0.

At that time over twenty-five years ago, only salmon fishers and tarpon anglers with a penchant for stunt fishing in the Tropics had any real cognizance of big-game fly fishing. Some might have had reels with better drags, but these were not in widespread use and they cost a king's ransom in the dollars of the time. I am convinced that I lost the world record for fly fishing with the "one that got away" and would have won that battle with the fly reel I use today. Modern fly-reel drags are as technologically advanced as the drags of both spinning and conventional reels.

In the same monster situation all the people standing around were using either 20-pound spinning or 50-pound conventional. It was a natural criticism for them to assume that I was fishing light because I was fly fishing, but I was not because no part of my tackle was less than 20-pound test. I did, however, lack the protection that a long section of mono in 20 pound would provide in stretch. There is no stretch in 2 feet of tippet.

If fly fishing for stripers from shore is going to gain acceptance, it is mandatory that strengths be realistically upgraded to compare with more traditional surfcasting methods. In the aforementioned anecdotes, in spite of violating IGFA fly-fishing limits of the time, I was able to beach those fish because I approached the maximum limits of the equipment. I might have even utilized a heavier tippet but I already knew that the fly-line strength—which I had no control over—might be insufficient. My tippet at 20 pound was protection for my fly line.

Had I been equipped with an extra spool, I might have continued fishing that night when I lost the monster. The myriad situations with which the fly fisher is confronted call for a collection of sink rates to suit, adjust, and otherwise comply with the ever-changing conditions of the shore. Certainly a second-choice sink rate is better than no fly line at all.

Dawn, the time when I caught the biggest striped bass I have ever taken fly fishing in my life, the 43-pounder, is magical in its ability to inspire great striper fishing. Dawn's failing, against the backdrop of the luxury and novelty of fishing in daylight, is that it is too short. We cannot lengthen the dawn, and no one goes fishing for one hour. Years ago someone asked me how to get more out of the dawn. I said, "Start fishing at midnight."

Flies and Moby Stripers

My experience with most big stripers on a fly is limited to those times when they wouldn't take anything else. For me fly fishing is held to the same standard as all my other activities in the field—it has to be the best way for the situation that confronts me. If there is one thing I fear, it is to be accused of fly-fishing for the wrong reasons. Never forget that I'm an eel fisher and plug caster whose youthful "fly fishing" for trout was done with a small tin of worms in my coolest pocket. Still, I think of myself as a friend of the craft because I practice my fly fishing with a utilitarian bent.

Big stripers on a fly, you ask? I have often taken the fly rod off the buggy roof because it was the only thing that had not been tried when selective bass would not cooperate. Both the 40-pound-plus stripers and many over 30 pounds that I took fly fishing fell into that category. Yet it is not the fish themselves that are a source of pride for me. It is that I had outdone the best surfcasters on the planet with what was called, at the time, "trout tackle." I always use decent hooks—3/0 to 4/0—with big bass around. Like bear hunters with squirrel guns, I get the feeling that most folks fish too light.

Any pattern would get its turn to be a bad fly, but I think the fly's edge is that it is a better way to imitate small baits such as sand eels. It is a better rendition than a Rebel is. Regulars all know that selective linesides are often won over by using small, picky stuff. My dealing with "picky" behavior at the time was six or seven white saddle feathers, though I admit to joining the ranks recently of those who support more realism in fly choice, which is another subject.

My fly-fishing successes, as well as those of my wife, Joyce, reflect what opportunity presented itself at the time. While she has never beached one over 23 pounds, we have both continued to land what might be regarded as a valid sampling. Last season, for instance, we took many 28- to 32-inch stripers—8- to 12-pound fish with a small sprinkling in the 20-pound class. I'm aware of the widespread frustration over sizes. People don't understand the dynamics of population and are impatient over waiting eighteen years for a 40-pounder to grow and twenty-plus years for a 50-pounder. They have even resorted to making excuses for the Atlantic, saying that the fish have lost their ability to come to size; I don't think so. Size is the next stone in the road. If I didn't believe that, I would never have written *The Trophy Striper.*

With any tackle, a 40-pounder is a tall order. Big clubs in the year 2002 with hundreds of members, most fishing from boats, could not land a solitary fish of that size. With fly fishing so small a part of the whole sport, you will not hear about many. Nevertheless, fly fishers who understand the striper surf will take a valid census of what is there. It is a case of knowing striper fishing; the fly fishing is the easy part.

The Worm Hatch

Worm hatches get a lot of attention from fly fishermen because only they can deliver something small enough to imitate a juvenile worm. A scant inch or so long, these little critters never travel alone. A "hatch" can occur at any time; I have seen them in May, August, and all months between. When it happens there will be a bazillion in the estuary where they appear. The large numbers of them contribute dramatically to the angling frustration that springs from those times when worms, bass, and fly fishers meet—always at night. Let me add my speculations to what I think happens to the junk science of fly fishing for striped bass worm-wise.

If there are a few bass and billions of hatched worms, you have zero chance of catching anything. If there are a few worms and many bass, a suitable worm pattern will make you feel like a sailor with a fresh paycheck in a Panama bordello. Toss a coin if there are a lot of worms and a lot of bass. I have seen it all and it is an event to which I would always be thankful to have been invited.

Phil Farnsworth, and you never forget someone who has given you a killer fly, handed me a rather boring-looking 1½-inch-long chunk of red velvet with a black head one night while fishing in Narragansett Bay. I would never pay money for a thing that simple, but it was free so I moved some other dead flies over and put it beside them in my fly wallet where it belonged. You have to know where I'm going with this, but stay with me for a bit regardless. Anyway, I rolled my eyes over this childish creation for at least four years, with no interest in using it because worm hatches crush my sense of expertise—and remember, I have written six striper books, which is a way of saying that I know something. The second week in June 2003, I found a worm hatch in Rhode Island. The orange little buggers were zinging this way and that, bass popping all around the estuary. I was not thrilled because I despise competition from the bait, but you take the conditions given to you. I protected my manhood adequately the first hour with a few schoolies, but as the night wore on, my hits came farther and farther apart and the slops, girgles, slashes, and smashes closer together. My score was slipping. Out of sheer desperation, I put Farnsworth's red velvet worm fly on my leader and proceeded to a steady pick that improved way over what I had been doing. It showed me that—even when they are on worms—there is always a better fly. It got me to thinking at the vise the next day while trying to apply red Magic Marker to white velvet, the only material I had for the project.

Years ago, during my love affair with sea-run browns, I discovered that black leeches were a favored forage for these tidewater sea trout. To imitate them I wrapped a black underbody, then added a tuft of black marabou. Pressing the marabou forward so as to make it hump, I tied it down and repeated the hump twice more. For the fourth hump, I tied it around the curvature of the hook so that the last part of the tuft was pointed downward. The forward stripping action on the retrieve caused the preloaded tuft to waggle up, creating the illusion of vertical undulations. The leach was a real killer and still is. How do you imitate a worm? Like a leech, although I admit that the similarities in movement between leeches and cinder worms may be a bit of a stretch. I had a large supply of orange marabou that I used to follow a leech-tying technique that really moves stripers to it. You should have seen what stripers thought of an orange-colored marabou cinder worm with vertical undulations as it moved through the estuary the following night. There is always the chance that the fish used in the trial would have taken anything, but I have been in on enough worm hatches to know about the failure they can cause. My marabou worm fly had the kind of inner life that you can envision from all those worm legs pumping at the same time, and I am convinced that "Frank's Cinder Worm" is a viable—if not legendary—pattern.

TYING FRANK'S CINDER WORM

Hook: 1 or 1/0 Mustad 34007 stainless hook

Thread: Danville's Black Flat Waxed Nylon or equivalent

Body: Medium or large orange chenille

Body/tail: Three 1½-inch tufts of orange blood marabou

Hackle: Hackle collar, black saddle

After tying the chenille underbody, pin the marabou at the throat of the fly. Then push the marabou forward to create a hump on top and pin it down with six or more turns of thread. Repeat this at least two more times. The last hump should be around the corner of the hook bend so that the tail points downward, creating a preload that will waggle upward when the fly moves forward. Wind the black thread to create a black head at the throat of the fly, add hackle, then whip-finish and lacquer. You will notice that the bushiness of marabou is quite pronounced, but the materials withdraw nicely. This makes it look very wormy when wet, taking on the slim form of the worm it is meant to simulate.

Out of desperation, I adapted my favorite trout fly for use as a cinder worm.

The Black Factor

Fishers are always asking about color in plug fishing as well as fly fishing, and the suspicion that colors matter dominates the imaginations of all that dabble in artificials.

Years ago while plug fishing, I found that many plugs did particularly well striper fishing at night. I cannot extrapolate any generalizations about "black at night/light during the day" or vice versa. Still, I do think that black has a stronger silhouette that can enhance its attention-drawing capabilities. Similarly, I was on a tide rip for an inlet only a few years ago using Clousers, and the black pattern was superior to those that were white or of a gradient in more natural colors. Remember that when it comes to the Owens Velvet Eel (see chapter 2), black is superior. Once I learned that the orange version of the old black leech used in sea-run browns was moving stripers, I went back to a striper-sized black leech on a 1/0 hook and did just as well. Whatever fly you use, start with black.

My wife, Joyce, with a worm hatch striper. The right fly fools them.

Don't Marry a Pattern

A common trap—and I know because it happens to me all the time—is to settle into the use of one fly, never fishing with anything else. We do this because the pattern becomes comfortable given the confidence we develop. The reputation for being *the* fly becomes self-fulfilling in that, after a while, you begin to think that because you catch all your stripers with this one fly, there is no need for others. For instance, forty years ago, when I utilized the white saddle eel fly, I used it so exclusively that I had no other patterns. I fished that one fly—changing only the hook size it was wound on—for ten years. It has only been the last few years, largely since the end of the striper moratorium, say 1990, that I began to lurk around the display counters of fly shops and experience crabs, shrimp, cinders, peanut bunker, and so forth capturing my fancy. Still, I keep getting involved in these love affairs with various patterns, springing from some bizarre combination of whimsy and luck. It seems only to take one good night—probably when they would have taken anything—to get the process of fly love and devotion into my bloodstream. I'm okay. Are you okay?

Something that needs further emphasis is that my methods, brags, and comparisons are of the *surf*. If you want to catch more stripers—fly fishing or otherwise—fish from a boat. Among many, I'm a proud surfcaster who never really knows if he is fishing wrong in an acre of stripers or right in an empty sea. Even if I could carry a graph recorder, I wouldn't have a place to plug it in anyway.

6

Where to Fly Fish for Stripers

(You'll love me for this.)

A curious social component is in place on the Striper Coast where certain locations are known for certain kinds of fishing. For instance, I fish some outflows today where the only anglers there are fly fishing. However, because I drifted live alewives there thirty years ago, I am aware that the spot does not have to be fly fished exclusively. When I went to Nauset Beach on Cape Cod for the first time over forty-five years ago, everyone I observed was fishing worms on the bottom and talking about how they used to plug fish there. The last time I was at Nauset, they were fishing sea worms, casting plugs, and fly fishing. A lesson that we can glean from the previous examples is that you can fish any way that you are accustomed for striped bass. I can think of no case to the contrary.

We all have to accommodate our individual differences in skill level when we choose to fish a certain shore with the fly. Certainly there are going to be times—day or night—when a raging surf, vicious onshore gale, crowds, cliffs, boat traffic, even temperatures will make fly fishing a poor choice of method for your surfcasting. Skilled fishers will function in greater adversity than others will. That said, my purpose in this chapter is to examine locations where most anglers will be comfortable presenting flies to striped bass.

I am going to touch upon some of the fly-fishing spots that I know about from New Jersey to the Maritimes. Nevertheless, before I begin, I want you to know that there are weaknesses in my familiarity with New

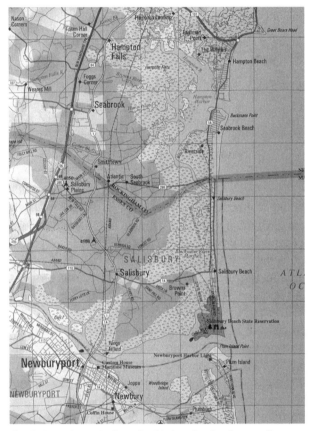

The Striper Coast is dotted with hundreds of great fly-fishing spots.

Jersey and Long Island. There are shore-fishing hot spots there that I can only speak from a commonsense point of view rather than any hard experience. Conversely, you will see the intimacy that I have with the shore from Watch Hill, Rhode Island, to Boston, Massachusetts, and how it diminishes again once I leave my backyard. I would need another forty years of roaming the Striper Coast to do it right and would love to get the chance. Lastly, if a particular state interests you, get one of DeLorme's map books for that state. Each costs less than twenty dollars and can save you a hundred in grief, a thousand in time.

New Jersey

As one of our more important surfcasting states, New Jersey offers a liberal number of bays or estuaries where shore fishing can be practiced. As along the rest of the coast, fly-fishing interest has grown to huge levels as people pile onto the striper explosion. Again, your fly-fishing opportunities would probably be best practiced at openings like a series of inlets in south Jersey: Hereford, Townsend's, Corson's, Absecon, and Brigantine all provide estuarine moving water with suitable back pond opportunities. Brigantine is not flanked by jetties and has a nice slow curving sand beach with a mix of sloughs and holes that can be waded and cast on a dropping tide.

Beach Haven Inlet (Hole Gate) is the south end of Long Beach Island. Currents are best at the inlet itself, although you can find fish anywhere along the last 3 miles. Don't restrict yourself to a dropping tide there because, with so much flow from Little Egg Harbor, you can fish any tide. This area is commonly fly fished.

At the north end of Long Beach Island is Barnegat Light, where crowds gather with spinning and conventional gear. The jetty there gets a little snotty at times and, as a result, I would not fly fish right there. In the back in the protected bay, I suspect there are some worthwhile explorations.

Island Beach State Park is best fished with an oversand vehicle, but a car can still be used on the road paralleling the beach. Island Beach utilizes a system of zoning the beach A-1 to A-23, about a quarter mile apart. Last that I knew, the best structure was A-6 to A-13. Three miles south of the park's entrance, the first beach access, open only during the nonbathing time, is the ever-popular Gillikin's Road. There should be another mile of nice bars, rips, and pockets. Generally the deeper water along Island Beach is at the north end; it gets shallower as you approach the inlet to Barnegat Bay, a jetty that is about 1½ miles on foot from the last parking area. This is another jetty that can get mean and watery and apparently is not fly-fishing suitable.

Sedge Island, which you don't actually fish from but face when looking west into Barnegat Bay, has a nice rip (Bulkhead) between the island and the shore of Long Beach Island. It is behind the last parking lot, but access is difficult from the lot, and most people fishing the Bulkhead go along the shore from the inlet. Outgoing tide is supposed to be the best, and this spot is traditionally fly fished.

There are a lot of jetties from Manasquan to Long Branch, and the surf fishing is good. Just how well fly fishers deal with the water there is dependent upon conditions and the individual's ability to handle those conditions.

Sandy Hook Point—which guards the opening to Raritan Bay—is shallow and offers a long wade; it is both plug and fly fished. I am not certain how well they do fly fishing, but the plug fishers clean up. You are looking at Staten Island and greater New York City.

New York

With the Hudson River supporting its own fishery, this whole area is striper water clear up the Hudson to Troy Dam. All the way north to that dam there are hundreds of small creeks, which have runs of bait-fish and provide fresh water to the stripers. I suspect, though I do not know for sure, that the best time for fishing in Hudson tributaries is spring, as the rest of the year bass are largely at sea.

All the inlets on the Long Island South Shore attract and hold stripers, starting with Breezy Point and heading east; however, most are flanked by jetties that are unsuitable as fly-fishing platforms. Regulars largely fish these areas from a buggy in the off season, and fly fishing can be carried out along the open beaches and in some of the backwater ponds. Beach permits are issued for oversand vehicles, de-pending upon jurisdictions. For instance, once you are clear of Jones Inlet (West End 2) there are 8 miles of drivable beach shared by Robert Moses State Park and Gateway National Seashore, and both require separate permits. Fire Island Inlet is the best of the fishing, but once the beach is open to driving after the bathing season it is watched closely by shore fishermen clear to Moriches Inlet. Fly fishers walk the back pond shore inside the inlet jetties and listen for slurping sounds, once the tide is down some.

Montauk is famous surfcasting water, and the crowds there are still outnumbered by the stripers and blues that frequent its stones. I just wonder if you might be better off fly fishing elsewhere, as I have never heard of it being done at Montauk.

Peconic Bay harbors some gorgeous and protected striper fishing, but I worry about suitable access for someone on foot fishing its shores. I have never fished there, but I would bet that it has its own secrets important enough to hear sighs of relief from those who do.

Connecticut

One of the reasons why saltwater fishing is largely carried out in boats in Connecticut is that access to the shore is limited by private property, illegally hidden rights-of-way, and discriminating local ordinances against access. Nowhere in New England is it more evident than on this overpopulated shoreline. Consequently, about all the legal shore-fishing access is designated as state park. A more dispassionate critic would probably regard the spots fished regularly as examples of "multiple use"—DEP-speak for activities other than fishing. Yet I cannot get over the notion that fishing was uppermost in the minds of those who chose the only public shore fishing they have. In my Connecticut travels, and having held any number of seminars on fly fishing the striper surf there, audiences were always packed with rabid people who engaged in it and advanced the notion that fly fishing is becoming a big deal.

Calf Pasture Point in South Norwalk has a productive bar in front of the town pier that you cannot wade out to until the tide is about halfway down. You will see plug and fly fishers working this water after dark—if it is any good—until the rising water drives them off. The drop has an edge because of the currents of the Norwalk River added to the tide.

Westport's Cedar Point and Compo Beach are adjacent and usually thought of as one spot. Cedar is more protected at the river mouth, which is the Saugatuck River, while Compo is more the open Sound. Fly fishers seem to prefer the moving water of the river mouth, while the bait dunkers are at Compo. This spot is a little better than Calf Pasture, and I would advise you to block out early May and late October on your calendar.

Penfield Reef is a rock-and-cobble sand spit in Fairfield that extends into Long Island Sound. It is locally popular with fly fishers, who fish the reef down on the dropping tide in waders. While in this area, I would advise any serious fly fisher to determine where all the fishing is at the tidewater edge of the Housatonic. Having heard of this on the Internet for years, I know they have some successful fly fishing for bass somewhere on the "Housey." Even if I knew exactly where I couldn't tell you, because someone would kill me if I wrote about it.

You can gain access to Charles Island in Milford by parking at Silver Sands State Park. A half-mile bar runs from the beach to the island, where regulars work the rips during the drop in tide. You can only get to Charles Island at low tide, and you had better know the tide, visibility, and direction (because fished right it will be dark). This is a popular place, but everything done here is for keeps, and it only takes a few minutes for a newbie to wish he had gone elsewhere.

Wherever you fish, stick with basics and fish at night. Shore fishing is tough enough.

Floating lines and streamers are fine for the rips between the mainland and island.

The Connecticut River is mostly fished from boats, although I know of many people who use a boat to travel around the river, get to their pet spots, then alight and wade in shoreline coves, stream mouths, and islands. The tidal estuary goes clear to Hartford, but they fish all the way to Enfield Dam until mid-June in spring. A second fishery is in play on the Massachusetts end all the way to the Holyoke Dam and the fish elevator. This major drainage, its source at the Canadian border, has runs of eels, white perch, salmon, shad, shrimp, worms, crabs—about anything that can swim, fly, crawl, or chirp. All that forage makes this river a major striper location, especially in spring. Don't overlook the rivers that feed the Connecticut, some so small you can't read their names on the map. With more nooks and crannies here than many places on the coastline, an entire book could be devoted to this area alone. At times tidewater sections at Old Saybrook and Old Lyme are loaded.

Cornfield Point in Old Saybrook can have parking problems, so discretion and timing are important in how much you can fish unnoticed. This rocky shore sticks out enough into the Sound that it would command some good fishing anyway, but during a dropping tide in the deep night, I would watch the mouth of the creek at Great Hammock Beach. Most of this faces the southwest, the prevailing summer wind, so keep your tackle choices in mind.

Marine Headquarters in Old Lyme is a locally popular fly-fishing mecca intended to be the answer to all the concerns that bedevil shore fishers. You are on state property, accessible twenty-four hours a day for the Connecticut River with wadable flats, and you can go clear to the mouth of the Lieutenant River. At midtide the water flies all through there, and the Connecticut is very narrow. Fly fishers leave the newly constructed fishing pier and work the shallows with a floating line. Popular patterns imitate river shiners, sperling, grass shrimp, and baby bunker. Watch for cinder worm hatches also, as this eelgrass-infested estuary is bound to have awesome foraging opportunities.

In Old Lyme there is a nice sandbar at Griswold Point that is about half a mile long, leading to the confluence of Black Hall River and the Connecticut. Water books through there, and the place is popular with fly fishers. This is one of those barrier-beach-type spots where on a full dropping tide gamefish breathe heavily while facing the current. You can pick this area out on a map as the outermost east bank of the Connecticut River mouth just below Great Island Wildlife Management Area. Parking is a problem; the only suitable location I know of is Sound View Beach parking lot, a couple of miles away. Still, a sharpie with a bike, imagination, friends, or a penchant for commando raids could really love this place. I rank this spot fly fishing's "Best-In-State."

Downstream of the Route 156 bridge in Niantic, the Niantic River provides some fast-water fishing where anglers can cast from the western bank of the river between the main bridge and the railroad bridge; there is also some good fly fishing below the railroad bridge on both banks. Again, dropping tides are popular, but if there are bass around don't overlook the rips that form up at the opening of the Niantic on the rising tide as well.

When I did research for my third book, *Striper Hot Spots: The 100 Top Surfcasting Locations from New Jersey to Maine* (which, at the moment, has been printed eight times), I had a cuts list of worthy places. While they did not make the book for space reasons, they are worth investigating:

- ➤ Greenwich Point Park, Stamford
- ➤ Shippan Point, Stamford
- ➤ Sherwood Island State Park, Westport
- ➤ Pleasure Beach/Town Pier, Bridgeport
- ➤ Long Beach, Stratford/Bridgeport
- ➤ Stratford Point, Stratford
- ➤ Power plant on the Housatonic, Devon
- ➤ Milford Harbor, east and west jetties
- ➤ Sandy Point, West Haven
- ➤ Rocky Neck State Park, Old Lyme
- ➤ Harkness Memorial State Park, Waterford
- ➤ Bluff Point State Park, Groton

Rhode Island

With a 400-mile coastline, this is a nice state to fish, and it has had way less recognition as a striper state than is deserved. Nonetheless, inhabitants from Connecticut and points west travel to the "Ocean

State" for its striper fishing. Rhode Island is the home of the Little Rhody Flyrodders, a group of dedicated striper fishers that has been in existence since after World War II. Consequently, several assumptions can be made regarding the striper fishing in general and fly fishing in particular: Plenty of folks fly fish for linesides, and there are enough places where it can be done to make it work.

If you park in Watch Hill and walk west down a dune trail for a mile, you will get to a spit that curves around north into Little Narragansett Bay called Napatree Point. At midtide, rising or falling, there is enough current to appeal to stripers. Area citizenry know the fishing is good here but, just like everywhere else, once you add a walk to a spot, interest falls off sharply. Just don't think if you find yourself alone that you have made a mistake.

The Rhode Island South Shore, Watch Hill to Matunuck, with only two slight rock interruptions at Quonny, is 18 miles of sand beach, dropping off sharply enough for fishing from the beach. After September 15 it can all be driven with an oversand vehicle, and during summer enough of it can be accessed for surf fishing to keep you busy well into your dotage. This south-facing beach is subject to plenty of onshore wind, and when the sou'west howls the surf can kick up enough to belie fly fishing; however, that happens only part of the time, and it is possible to fly fish the open beach six nights out of seven. Stick around, because I have plenty of places around for you that one bad night. Generally I like extra-fast-sinking lines on the open beach with just about any streamer pattern. When bass are that close to shore, they are feeding. Of course, if you know something of the bait—and the September mullet and snapper blue runs can be memorable—go with your intuitions pattern-wise.

Let's do the three breachways in one breath because there is a lot here and I have to get back to the water. I don't suggest that you fly fish the three great pond openings from the jetties—or "breachways" as they are called in the Ocean State. The reason for this is that you will be high above the water on slippery rocks, nearly always among crowds of surfcasters using gear that is out of harmony with fly fishing and subject, if you do hook a moby striper, to vicious currents while fighting it. It is the back ponds that permit you to get even with the gorillas fishing the jetty ends. Weekapaug Breachway has the weakest currents and the poorest potential for fishing; keep right on going. Two crow miles east at Quonnie, it is possible to wade into the back pond where the breachway empties or fills, tide depending. You need a buggy for back pond access on the western side of the breachway, but a car is fine on the east bank. Take West Beach Road from Route 1 and follow your nose for 2 miles to a state launch ramp and parking area. As you face the tidal pond to your north, there will be a jetty-flanked opening where the water goes fast twenty hours per day on your left. Straight north and slightly right, currents on your left, there is a long wadable flat where you can hit the current and channel with your fly when facing west. Bass are not always there but, some nights, they can be banging away in frenzy on sperling, shrimp, or cinders. Years ago a local guide made this place popular, but he went out of business, most likely because once his charges found out how easy it was to fish these flats, they didn't need him anymore. The thing you have to watch out for here—in addition to the usual fog concerns or being run down by a boat—is avoiding have a moby striper foul you on the anchor lines of the navigation buoys. Give yourself as much room as possible by getting downtide of one. This is shallow water, and a floating line will catch stripers.

Similarly, Charlestown Breachway—we are following the coast north and east here—has some nice back pond shallows that make up on both tides where the actual breachway ditch dumps or draws with the pond. The rising tide seems to have an edge drawing pond stripers—and they are not always small—to where water comes into the pond. It is kind of a no-brainer in the application-of-water sense, but it is what I do. The only thing about Charlestown Breachway is that there are more boats than at any of the other places, and the boat traffic puts the fish down somewhat. For that reason the deep night during the week has an edge. In both cases, be mindful of the lag in tide in both these openings. At Quonnie flow ends two hours after the tide chart high tide, and at Charlestown Breachway, moon phase depending, at least three hours. Thus, with a midnight high, water will still be rising into the back pond until 3 AM.

You can't fish these two—Quonnie and Charlestown—without making comparisons in their hydrology. Quonnie Breachway serves a much smaller pond but is short and straight, permitting a healthier exchange of water. Charlestown Breachway, on the other hand, serves a larger pond in Ninigret Pond, but the feeder opening is long and winding, weakening the exchange of water. Thus, even though Quonnie appears to be at a disadvantage, it flows stronger and sends out a stronger, more easily detected current than the one at Charlestown.

In the straightness of the Rhody South Shore, Matunuck has a nice interruption in the formation of Carpenter's Bar and Deep Hole, two places—if the sou'west is not taking your breath away—that are adjacent and hold stripers reliably.

On the east shore of the Harbor of Refuge, if you follow Succotash Road to its bitter end there are pulloffs in the eelgrass where you can park and follow paths to the salt pond. There is wading on the flats all along them, and you can pick up bass moving into the pond with the tide. At the north end of the flat, there is a nice outflow from Potter Pond during the drop that sometimes has fish.

The south edge of the mouth of Narrow River (Pettaquamscutt River) in Narragansett can be accessed from Narragansett Town Beach on Ocean Road, Route 1. I have hit them both at high tide, water right to left, and at dead-low tide out beside River Rock. As an-

Out on a salt flat in the deep night, striper fishing is in its most primitive form.

other of those places that starts looking changed at different tides, once the tide is down, fish are confined to the much smaller main current. This is a well-known hot spot with locals, but you have half a chance of privacy in the deep night. Potential for cows here.

Up in Narragansett Bay, just north of Rome Point there is a nice outflow from an estuary behind Hamilton Beach. On moon tides the access road along the beach floods at high tide, which is any high tide in the evening. You cannot even drive out there until the tide is down an hour. By then neighborhood fish will be taking up positions in the current.

East of Goddard Park in the Potowomut section of East Greenwich, you can access Sandy Point, which commands a narrow section to the opening of Greenwich Bay. Here a bar hooks from east to south, and shore fishers line up on the bar the last three hours of the incoming. Bay waters rush into Greenwich Bay with a hard right-to-left current. This spot was made famous by weakfish (squeteague) runs those years when they were high enough in their cycle to venture north, but we have had some good striper and bluefish sunsets here. Providence moon tides offer a high at 8:30, so a perfect night here would be a 10 PM high.

Another incoming location is Conimicut Point, where a bar reaches out into the bay at a narrow spot across from Barrington, sort of guarding the opening to the Providence River. Duck hunters and shore fishers alike have in the past been swept off this bar and killed, and the water on either side of the bar is deep. Be conscious of the tide and hazards here. Better yet, fish it in the day.

Across the Providence River in Riverside, Sabin Point offers a similar situation where a bar reaches out into the bay, creates a line of foam, marking a drop-off where all gamefish—stripers, blues, and weakfish—can be found. Sabin Point is a park, and I have never been bothered fishing there.

On Barrington's Wompanoag Trail, northbound lane, Route 114, there is a large eelgrass estuary known as 100 Acre Cove. On the pulloff you will see that it is a "residents only" park, but if you are willing to risk a scolding from the local enforcement, the fishing directly east a few hundred yards over firm marsh grass is another of those narrows situations. I prefer the rise at midtide. It can be somewhat of a crap shoot, but I have occasionally hit them here.

Two rivers command the eastern side of Narragansett Bay—the Barrington, which we just left, and the Warren River, a few miles down

Route 114. The Warren is the second set of bridges. On that second bridge, if you look north you will see that the river opens into a big salt pond, with a marsh on the right. Again, if you forage for suitable neighborhood parking, which you should have improved on while in Connecticut, you can walk the marsh shore north toward the pond. Plenty of current and safe wading all the way to the point to the north, maybe 400 yards. It is deep enough to drown but shallow enough for a floating line. Very riverine, very much like you are fishing in a fjord; I have fished here since I was a kid and have caught bass, up to 35 pounds, with every imaginable method.

In Bristol, Colt State Park is a nice place to go to, and it has Mill Gut, a rip that forms on the drop from a hot-looking estuary. Still, I hesitate to recommend this place because it is closed to night access, and you may as well have a cookout as fish it in the daytime.

East across the Bristol peninsula at the end of Narrows Road off Route 136 are the Bristol Narrows. Late in the drop you can drive out onto a bar with any car because the bottom is firm. Once the tide starts in, I hope your car starts or your Mercedes will become an artificial reef. This spot is popular because of the currents that form up. It is very open for casting and reasonably wadable before the drop-off. Because this is a protected part of Mount Hope Bay, there is no surf and it has that popular river feel we all like.

BLOCK ISLAND

More famous for its other types of surf fishing, the "Block," as it is so fondly called, does have some fly fishing, as does every other location in this book. My memory of Sandy Point would make it a likely candidate for a Deep-Water Express or leadcore because of the dramatic drop-off it has. However, Sandy Point is far safer for people fishing from boats than it is for those fishing at night from shore. A little extra current, a rogue wave, and you are going to either Portugal or Montauk. This spot is a finger of sand that reaches out into the Atlantic at the extreme north end of the island, several hundred yards dipping slowly into the foam of a gigantic rip with blue water on both sides. You are gone if you trip, misjudge, or even sneeze. Strange thing about this spot is that it appears as attractive to gamefish as anyplace you will ever see, but I have never caught anything there even though the boats tonged on every drift. Let's go somewhere else.

The inlet to Great Salt Pond, also known as "The Cut," is the salt pond into New Harbor; it is considered the best shore-fishing spot on the island. Popular with fly anglers and pluggers, it is fished beginning at the jetty on the south side of the harbor opening, southeast along the shore for a good half mile toward Champlins Dock. The target species is striped bass, which you are more likely to catch, but they also get bluefish, bonito, and even little tunny some years. Don't know where I learned it, but the new epoxy patterns wreak havoc on the bonito here.

Massachusetts

MARTHA'S VINEYARD

Access to Vineyard hot spots varies with time and local politics, bird breeding, and local penchant for greater regulation. Places like Cape Poge, Wasque, much of the southern shore that is under private ownership muddy up the access picture. A glance at the map and you can see that there are enough places where the fly fishing at night would be memorable. Certainly there are enough bay and pond openings to keep it interesting, and there is way more potential for the fly fisher at these places than the open beaches. I have been to the Vineyard, but I am not intimate with it the way an islander might be. From what I do know surfcasters enjoy the Derby each fall September 15 to October 15, and there is a fly-fishing category in the competition. Here is what I have in safe approach, if you promise not to complain about how little experience I have here.

On the northeast shore on the Edgartown–Oak Bluffs Road, there is a barrier beach called the Joseph Sylvia State Beach separating a salt marsh and Sengekontacket Pond. Two bridges serve the openings that refresh the pond. Nearer to Oak Bluffs is Little Bridge, and a mile south is Anthiers Bridge. Both enjoy heavy current on either side of the bridges. Gentle surf, access to the back ponds, and prodigious currents all call loudly to island fly fishers. Better yet, the road paralleling the state beach gives people with a car the same advantages as those with a beach buggy on other shores in that they can stop nearly anywhere along the way to fish the beach. My old friend and original contact, the late Dr. Robert Post, who authored a fine Vineyard book called *Reading the Water,* once showed me the pond there. He said that it was occasionally loaded with sand eels and worm hatches; you might keep that in mind while either fishing the back shores or flanking jetties.

Gay Head is another spot you can drive to without a buggy for some reliable fly fishing at the southwest corner of the island. The opening to Menemsha Pond is considered one of the premier fly-fishing spots on the East Coast. Menemsha bight is located between Dogfish Bar and the jetty opening to Menemsha Pond. If there is suitable bait, the entire area will heat up, including the pond itself.

NANTUCKET

I know even less about Nantucket than the Vineyard. I was a guest there for plug fishing a few years ago and recall fishing the ever-popular south, which had a similar shore and surf to those of Rhode Island. We fished Smith Point at the western end of the beach, and there was good current and a suitably made-up beach and rip for what would have been good fly fishing. I also noticed that most beach buggies had a fly rod on the roof, which was reassuring. Stripers are taken reliably there both June and fall, but I wonder about midsummer. It seems that blues, albies, and bonito draw a lot of fly-fishing interest to the island in summer.

Brant Point, walking distance from the Nantucket ferry docking location, is very popular with bait fishers and would have to have some potential for fly fishing because of its command of the harbor entrance. It is about the only place on the island with which I'm familiar where you can fly fish without a buggy. There are also fewer estuarine openings here than on the Vineyard.

Eel Point/Knuckles (Dionis) on the northwest shore is a quieter and more protected structure. However, once around the bend of Eel Point into Madaket Harbor, you are back into the teeth of the prevailing sou'west. There is a lot of flats wading here once the tide is down enough after dark, and fly fishers do well. Just don't work this area during fog or without a compass. If the tide is too high, fish Eel Point until it is down enough for Madaket.

Great Point, on the northeast corner of Nantucket, enjoys a collision of currents from all directions, and the sea there kicks up something like you will see in few other spots. Permits are sold for driving out there. Still, I have serious doubts about fly fishing this area, because often its famous results are accomplished with outrageous casting distances best accomplished with a potato gun. Let's head for firmer ground.

SOUTHERN MAINLAND MASSACHUSETTS

The first Bay State hot spot moving north is the Westport River, with two branches. The dominant East Branch has the greater flow, more accessibility, and the better fishing as a result; both branches have many acres of eelgrass on their shores. Also, the water is clean and the flow attracts as well as holds good numbers of bass. I caught my first 52-pounder here with a surf rod in 1964, and you never forget such a memorable occurrence. It is somewhat of a challenge to move around the river on foot because of the marshes, but it is a great place for kayaking to spots where you can fish in waders. We always did well off the islands above the Route 88 bridge. Just before Route 88 hits the water, state-owned Horseneck Beach is on the right. This 2-mile shore is loaded with beachy structure produced by the outflowing currents of the river, containing a lot of nice holding water.

From Westport to Buzzards Bay, there are many locally important locations on both banks that include the western Cape from the canal to Woods Hole. Points, islands, coves, harbors, and river mouths dot the seascape, providing a variety of structure.

The Cape Cod Canal's reputation for stripers has been built on heavy casting tackle, long casts, and deep runs with fast-sinking metal. Only a few suitable spots for fly casting are offered here as a result. Pip's Rip at the eastern end of the mainland side provides some opportunity at low tide on the Boston chart. It is also possible to wade east at low tide toward Cape Cod Bay and find breaking fish, particularly at daybreak. Another less reliable canal option is the Mud Flats on the western end of the Cape side. It is also possible to take bass in the shadows of bridge abutments by having your fly drift along the edge of the shadow edge.

CAPE COD

Oversand vehicle permits for beach buggies are issued for Sandy Neck, managed by the town of Sandwich. Those not wanting to use a beach vehicle can also fish the mouth of Scorton Creek from the western side. With an ORV, at the extreme east end of the beach, there is a much larger and wider outflow from Barnstable Harbor. Currents here can be fished on both tides. The harbor is a breeding ground for baitfish and draws bass up from Cape Cod Bay.

Probably the best location on the Cape not requiring the use of a buggy is Chatham Inlet, which includes the beach of South Island fishable at any tide. During night hours you can park in the town lot across from the Chatham Lighthouse and walk down to the inlet. The key to making this spot work for you is low tide after dark. Plan on fishing two hours on either side of low on the Boston chart. During this period, the only bass movement in and out of Pleasant Bay has to be done in the channel right at your feet. It is the time when stripers are most vulnerable to angling. A similar situation, though on a smaller scale, is at Stage Harbor mouth to the south.

A number of guides operate flats-fishing services in Chatham and take fly fishers out to Monomoy by boat in the daytime. Some of this is wading and some is carried on from the boats. Contemporary Monomoy regulars all rave about fishing there, which is very different: It is sight fishing in the day, exciting in what you will see, and often frustrating. Regulars feel that bass have seen all the patterns; even so, small crabs and shrimp flies seem best. When we fished Nauset Beach's Chatham Inlet years ago before the Nauset breakthrough, Monomoy waters were considered the sacred land of dream striper fishing, and I see no reason why that would change.

Nauset Beach in Orleans has a parking lot used by on-foot anglers during the night. While it is possible to catch bass along the beach in either direction, I believe north or left is a better choice because the nearer you get to Nauset Inlet, the more the inlet influences the adjacent shore. Once you get to where you can see rocks in the water—and there are few rocks on Cape Cod—you are at Gorilla Hole, where big bass are caught. Keep in mind that surf and depth here will test your fly-fishing skills. Another mile north and you will have Nauset Inlet where bass trade in and out. Don't overlook the back pond estuary.

For the buggy-equipped surfcaster, the governing towns of Orleans and Chatham issue permits for buggies. Structure along Nauset Beach, which is highly variable in intensity and mix from one season to another, can be exciting some years and not worth the permit others. Note the structure during low tide and pick out the places you want to home in on. Of course the south end of the beach, which is the north lip of the same Chatham Inlet above, is a local hot spot that pays off all through the rise in tide with currents heading for Pleasant Bay. The proximity you can drive to the inlet is restricted, with the distance variable season to season, but it won't kill you.

The entire Outer Cape on its east or Back Beach side holds stripers and provides memorable fly fishing all summer as well as way later into fall than most realize. Administrators of the national seashore issue parking permits for night hours for people equipped to fish. They can be used at any number of parking areas spaced north along the outside. All the towns, starting with Eastham, offer access to the north side of Nauset Inlet, and each one gets a turn at providing monster striper fishing. This is the area that served as model for the earlier chapter on beach reading; you will find bar corners, finger bars reaching seaward, and sloughs leading into and out of holes.

I am not sure how much junk science is in my theory, but I have always felt that the Outer Cape really does not come into its own until the bluefish arrive at the Race and drive the bass out, usually early August. With prevailing winds out of the southwest, coming right over the dunes, there is a gentle wave action that does not interfere with fly fishing, and this is all pleasant going as long as the water is clean and clear.

At High Head, just above Highland Light, a red weed locally called mung (but it's not pollution) infests the shoreline so badly that much of the area above Cape Cod Light (Highland Light) is unfishable. While distressing, it fades quickly as you get closer to the lighthouse. However, the north or any eastern quadrants of wind will push this awful red gunk south to the point that it can shut down all fishing. The longer the errant winds bluster, the farther south this disgusting stuff goes. Linestorms, nor'easters, and hurricanes all do their part in saving striped bass. Some years, just when the mung cleans up a little, along comes another blow and you have to start the cleanup clock all over again.

In Provincetown from High Head northwest around the Cape's hook to Race Point Light, you are a little safer from the red weed. One apparent reason is that the currents are stronger, and they combine with prevailing winds to sweep it cleaner sooner. Surf is so gentle here most of the time that you can fish this shore in hip boots. You will still want waders for going out on the bars. While there are fewer bars, they can be very good, and you should mark them at low tide. Remember that Race Point guards the opening to Cape Cod Bay, and the first 3 miles of beach east of Race Point Station is influenced by that filling and emptying of the bay.

Race Bar does fill up with bait fishers, but if you can find room to fly cast, you can have some marvelous fishing here on stripers that are pigging on sand eels. My biggest fly-fishing stripers—two over 40 pounds—were taken here at low tide when bass were rooting for sand eels. (See chapter 5, "Situations That Teach.") After the tide starts its noticeable rise, head a couple of hundred yards east to a spot commonly called the Traps, as the fish will line up there to face the current. Admittedly most of my Traps blitzes were with casting gear, but on one occasion I embarrassed traditional Cape surf fishermen with—what did they call it?—"A fooking trout pole."

At the bitter end of Route 6, called Herring Cove or New Beach, you can get a parking permit from the seashore and walk this southwest-facing shore. I would use a fast-sinking line and sand eel imitation without worrying too much about distance, because if the bass are playing around here they will be panning sand eels right at the shore edge, and your best action will come casting down the beach. You can go north toward Race Light, which you cannot miss on foot, until you reach the opening to Hatches Harbor. Or you can go south toward Wood End. It all has great potential.

Again, without a buggy, you can park around the Provincetown Inn and go out on the dike or breakwater and find a place where the water leaks through the stones. It is best on the dropping tide for that reason. If they are there you will hear them.

The Pamet River, which is inside Cape Cod Bay in North Truro, is an estuarine outflow draining miles of marsh. Again, the falling tide is the ticket, you don't need a buggy, and the walk is under half a mile. Breakwaters guard the opening but, once the tide is down, there is wading out front that reaches the outflow currents.

GREATER BOSTON

All the towns south of Boston have locally important estuaries and beaches, but they have set up a system of "residents only" parking devised to exclude outsiders. This is the same sort of thing that forced Connecticut's purchase of more desirable coastal property for the public. Only little of that is done in Massachusetts, and access is a problem in the area. If you want to paint your face in eelgrass camo and do your fishing like a commando, the North River is a nice estuary that draws bass. No doubt there are others, but I hate ending a night with having my car towed.

Boston Harbor, since it has been cleaned up by multibillion-dollar sewage treatment, is a garland of islands separated by rips of clean water. Places like those islands connected by bridges—Deer, Moon, and Long Islands—can be driven and fished from shore. Since the harbor cleanup a number of charter boats specializing in fly fishing have sprung up and garnered good reputations.

The best fly fishing in the Plum Island vicinity is Joppa Flats, which is an upriver location on the Merrimack River; these flats are adjacent to a vast acreage of eelgrass, and Newyburyport hosts countless hard-cores who wade these tidal flats in search of great numbers of bass. I would assume that floating lines are best here because the water is shallow enough for wading. However, I would not venture out onto the flats without an experienced local "flatlandah" who knows how the tide works here, as it is a long way and you don't want to get turned around so far from shore. Problems develop nights when the fishing is good and casters forget about timing.

New Hampshire

Hampton River Inlet, a mile-plus tidal estuary for the Hampton River, can be fished on either bank from Route 1A. Best fly fishing is the protected estuary in the back, where there is plenty of wading. As a state park, there is parking on both sides of the bridge. At night, or in the early morning, they won't bother you when fishing. If you get above the bridge and fish the rapidly building currents of falling water and hook a good fish, it will try to go under the bridge and you will be in trouble, so think all that out before you start casting.

New Hampshire's short coastline is compensated for by the vastness and structural variety of Great Bay, a 15-mile estuary with plenty of protected fly-fishing water. Having never fly fished the bay, I only know that these waters provide striper opportunities consistent with bass populations on the rest of the Striper Coast. Boat fishing there is robust, so the shores—where access is legal—would have to follow.

Maine

Note that as I get farther from my home waters, a certain intimacy with the fishing begins to decline. I have fished all the places mentioned here at one time or another, but I lack the many nights needed to truly unravel a spot's secrets. That takes years. Nevertheless, in general terms, something comes through regarding postmoratorium striper fishing: Maine's striper fishing reflects the return of bass. It is somewhat of a miracle if you go to any outflow during the drop in tide at night and do not find stripers. Also, and I cannot be sure why, fishing in many of Maine's fjords has provided more day fishing opportunities than I have experience elsewhere.

Access to Maine's coastal fishing is largely open, even on private property. What little posted land you will find there is owned by outsiders who came from elsewhere and brought their land-sharing attitudes with them.

Angling traditions here tend to be more in freshwater trout and salmon. Fly fishing, on the other hand, is the only way to fish for many, and now that word is out on striper fishing the two have come together much in the way that I try to tie both disciplines together in this book. Like me, Mainers who tasted the adventure of seeing their backing on a "salmon" river have sought to reignite that challenging experience in tidewater. The logic in the connection is universal. Let's scratch the surface of Maine's most obvious fly-fishing choices, leaving a few for the joys of exploration.

The Mousam River in Kennebunkport drains an eelgrass-laden marsh at its mouth. This is a small spot that retains its flow at all but the top of the flood. As with any inlet, try to determine what forage is in the estuary before choosing a pattern. With nothing else to go by, select any reliable streamer that you trust for flats wading the tail end of the drop.

The Saco's 4 miles of tidal river upstream to Biddeford/Saco is wide water that is fished heavily from boats. Still, one look at this little bay and you can see that it is striper water. Most of the fly fishing here, because of the depths and currents, would be best done with an extra-fast-sinking line and, because of the enormity of the "river," even a shooting head. I have not fished all of it, but I was very impressed with the Biddeford Pool, and reports are always being published about salmon fishermen being bothered by stripers under the first dam way upstream. Kind of a no-brainer, the Saco River may be Maine's—when measured per mile—best striper river. Good protection in here if you want to fish during a storm.

The Scarboro River, with its customary, Maine-like, minimal half-mile border of eelgrass, is a huge salt marsh. If you are ever around at daybreak during a falling tide, you can see bass breaking as they go out with the tide. Because of all the marsh grass, moon tides tend to produce floating grass that can foul your line. Also, access, which used to be a railroad bed from Pine Point Road next to Snow's Cannery, has

Day fishing on the Maine coast, our daughter Susan sees more stripers than fishermen.

been closed off to driving, and the walk is just under a mile. There is a fork to the estuary; the side on the east is bigger, usually with more water and bass all over it. (I think the fish are there to eat mosquitoes, which are the size of teal.) If you are a kayaker, you could crawl all over this place with no effort.

The mouth of the Spurwink River at Higgins Beach has been loaded with small stripers every time I have ever been there. A small river, you can wade the sand bottom right on the beach at the outflow. The lower the tide the better, and, if it is down very far and still dark, you likely will hook up on every cast. Leave your vehicle at the general store and walk half a mile, because officials don't want anyone parking at Higgins Beach.

Popham Beach in Phippsburg is state property, and there is ample parking. You will see every manner of fishing, from chunking the bottom to plug fishing. Water moves briskly through here because this cove at the fort is also the mouth of the Kennebec. I feel that a sinking line is your best choice, because water is deep and tidal exchanges are robust. You do not see much fly fishing here, but everything else is done so why not?

With a floating line you're better off at the Morse River a mile west on Route 209. This smaller estuary has good currents, flats wading, little to no boat traffic, and offers fishing in a thinner water column. I am not sure what it is about this spot, but Morse River stripers are stupid, which are my kind of bass. You don't have to know anything.

I have not been fishing in Augusta since the breaching of Edwards Dam, but time was when bass up to 20 pounds could be taken in the state capital. Again, it was always the salmon fishermen who cursed the linesides for taking their flies. (In that world anything that is not a salmon is a rough fish suitable only for fertilizing tomatoes.) All the salmon rivers have varying levels of stripers that mix right in with the salmon, so you really don't know what you have the first few seconds of a take. The Kennebec River has its own successfully reproducing native strain of striped bass. It will be interesting to see what the added water they now access to Waterville will do for the population.

Where does Maine striper fishing end? Being as I am a flatlander, I have told you all that I know and have not touched a thousandth of what there is. Nor does it end in Maine, as migratory stripers are commonly fished to the end of November in Nova Scotia's Minus Basin—

a spot in a place where I know even less about. Let me share an interesting thing about Nova Scotia stripers, lest you think they don't grow well. The official record striped bass is over 54 pounds taken in 1994, and the unofficial record over 57 pounds. To think I once thought theirs was all schoolie fishing.

So many striper hot spots, so little time.

Frank's Top Ten Spots— South to North

1. Sedge Island, Island Beach State Park, New Jersey

2. West End 2, Long Island

3. Griswold Point, Connecticut

4. Narrow River Inlet, Narragansett, Rhode Island

5. Inlet to Great Salt Pond, Block Island, Rhode Island

6. Smith Point, Nantucket, Massachusetts

7. Chatham Inlet, Cape Cod, Massachusetts

8. Race Point to Wood End, Cape Cod, Massachusetts

9. Joppa Flats, Newburyport, Massachusetts

10. Morse River, Phippsburg, Maine

7

Natural History of Striped Bass

Whatever is known about striped bass *(Morone saxatilis)* was not learned in sportfishing with a fly. Hands down, over 99 percent of what has been fathomed, learned by accident, or gleaned from the growing body of scientific journals occurred as a result of fishing from boats or casting from the beach. Indeed, we can attribute little of what is known about this great gamefish to fly fishing. When measured against the years sportfishers have pursued stripers, fly fishing is still in its infancy; little really exists—by comparison—in the body of knowledge that pertains to fly fishing the striper surf. However, there is enough useful information about the species to draw productive conclusions.

Populations

Three races of striped bass embody most of the migratory bass of the Northwest Atlantic—what I call the Striper Coast: the southern, consisting of Chesapeake tributaries and other, mostly Virginia, rivers; the

Hudson, which old research said produced 10 percent of the total population of Northwest Atlantic bass; and the Delaware River, newest contributor to the burgeoning bass population, kicking in an unknown number of stripers. Since the postmoratorium return of linesides, a number of small ancillary striper populations have sprung up in places where formerly they had never existed. This, no doubt, is the result of anomalies in bass distribution that are bound to happen when the numbers are up. Bigger streams, like the Connecticut River, are thought to be producing juveniles. Winter-over populations are occurring in spots where they have not been seen in years, such as the Providence River and Cape Cod's Scorton Creek. Not that these are important, but they serve to shore up the argument that more striper anomalies happen when there are more fish.

MEASURING POPULATIONS

The two largest sources of stripers, the southern and Hudson, each utilize a scientific means of measuring the spawning success of the season known as the young-of-the-year index (YOY). The larger, crucially important Maryland index is determined by averaging the number of juvenile bass found in three rounds of seining at twenty-two sites on the Chesapeake Bay. The highest ever recorded, for the sixty-six samples at this writing, was fifty-nine in 1996; the lowest, under one in 1981. Fisheries managers generally consider anything above eight to be a good spawning year. As you can see examining these YOY numbers, seasons suffer from wildly variable levels of spawning success.

A natural consequence is that these varying spawn years produce long-term fluctuations in size opportunity after the passing of suitable years. This explains why we might have a glut of immature schoolies 12 inches long one year, then five years later, taking into account natural mortality and known rates of growth, a preponderance of 24-inch 5-pounders. Such dominant year-classes simply reflect what was born before and can be predicted through the known rates of growth, long understood by the scientific community.

These variations in fecundity cause dramatic changes in size and number of available bass from one year to the next. Such dominant year-classes bring some predictability of both size and numbers,

The striper is back in spades and can be taken with a variety of methods.

telling us we are entering a period of the kind of large-striper fishing opportunity that was last experienced in the 1970s.

Striper Size

Once you understand the combined dynamics of dominant year-class and rates of growth, it is fairly easy to predict your chances for certain sizes of bass. Therefore, when you mull your chances of catching, say, a 50-pounder, what comes to mind is that the opportunity for such a fish could never be constant. Anglers who have sought to study such fish and the opportunity to catch them—and I have been one of those people since my first "fifty" in 1964—learn quickly that the opportunity for such a dream fish could not be, nor has it ever been, historically constant. For instance, in the late 1960s there were roughly two-hundred-plus such fish taken coastwide by all methods; in the early postmoratorium years of the 1990s, less than five per season. The 2002 season, measured roughly and unscientifically because there is no august body that maintains such statistics, produced over twenty. In the summer of 2003, as I write this midseason, there have already been forty-five 50-pounders, which—even if no other is caught—will be a postmoratorium record.

When people seek to trivialize the so-called good old days of moby striper fishing, saying it was easy then, they should be reminded that a "fifty" varies from one in a million to one in a hundred thousand. Generally 10 percent of a year's catch might come from the beach. No 50-pounder, as far as I know, has ever been taken fly fishing from shore.

Sixty-pounders, and I have only seen one in my life, caught only yards away on a small plug with light tackle on Nauset Beach, make up 1 or 2 percent of the stripers that exceed 50 pounds any given year. Nevertheless, in 1967 there were twelve 60-pounders out of 152 over 50. That season, the first 70-pound-plus in fifty-four years, taken by Charles E. Cinto, was sport caught. There has been a spate of 70-pounders since then over the last twenty years, topping off with the current all-tackle world record, a 78½-pounder by Albert R. McReynolds. The wonder of it was that he used light tackle on a wild night on the New Jersey shore fishing a Rebel.

Historical accounts of commercially taken behemoths are strewn about in the literature. Haul seiner Ted Lester took a 78-pounder on Long Island ahead of McReynolds's record bass. The Nauset Beach parking lot used to have a commemorative plaque for a 91-pounder taken in the late nineteenth century with a handline by a surfcaster heaving and hauling a cod drail from the beach. (And you thought *you* fished the hard way with that "trout pole.") I cannot remember where I read it, but there was supposed to have been a 112-pounder taken off Orleans, the same Nauset Beach area, again in the late 1800s. Huge bass, it has long been known, lie in a staging area in winter off North

Carolina. Authors Bigelow and Schroeder refer to this in their fine scientific contribution, *Fishes of the Gulf of Maine:* "Several of about 125 pounds were taken . . . [in] 1891."

Brooklyn, New York, surf fisherman Gus Piazza, who also happened to work on the Fulton Street Fish Market floor, bought an 81-pounder for twenty dollars to have mounted for posterity. He told me that the shipment was from the South, probably North Carolina, and that there was a pair of 72-pounders in with the big one. He also convinced the Schaefer Brewery people in New York—who always had an interest in striper fishing—to front the cost of mounting it. Making the rounds of sport shows for years, it ended up being sold to a New Jersey restaurant for a thousand dollars. At least it was a state where stripers are celebrated—no, *worshiped.*

1967 WAS MEMORABLE

Charles E. Cinto's 73-pounder, the first 70-plus in fifty-four years after Charles Church's original 73-pound world record, fell to a trolled plug at Cuttyhunk in 1967. The 1 or 2 percent rule of 60-pounders was

While not fly caught, Charles E. Cinto with a 73-pound striper illustrates what's out there in wild stripers.

thrown askew when the Schaefer Brewery counted their awards with twelve 60-pounders out of 152 over 50—again, 1967. It was also the year that Piazza found the 81-pounder and the two 72-pounders. My third 50-pound-plus, a mere 51 pounds beached in late July of that season, helps relieve the notion that I might have missed something, but there is a big difference between 51 and 81 pounds. Let's get away from this digression and explain big fish further.

OTHER SIZE INFLUENCES

Along with wanting you to understand that striped bass grow way bigger than the ones caught sportfishing, these moby fish are nearly thirty years old. A 50-pounder is over twenty years of age. They are certain to be females, because males rarely exceed 15 pounds and the largest known male weighed 40. Individual condition plays in; as with every animal on the planet, some may have a genetic propensity for greater size. You will sometimes beach a nice striper that has pigged so heavily on bait that it sags heavier than a lifetime beer drinker. This is more likely to happen in fall, when the sea like the land is lush with nourishment, you have a few-pounds advantage in your quest for bragging rights that does count in the measurement of a trophy lineside.

With the great number of stripers in the Northwest Atlantic, there is a growing sentiment that bass exhibit poorer growth than they did years ago. I do not know if this is some twisted notion meant to trivialize the great fish of years past, or if those who believe this really think a million years of adaptation and natural selection could be altered in twenty-five years. Misunderstandings of the "inch-per-pound" rule has some saying that "in the old days a 40-inch bass weighed 40 pounds" are nothing more than the extension of the same notion that a 50-pounder weighs an inch per pound. The only point on the size continuum where they weigh an inch per pound is right at 50 to 52 pounds. Forty-inch stripers usually weigh less than 25. They always did. Another factor that blends in some inaccuracy in observations about the then-and-now in striper measurement is that old-guard striper measurements were required then to be fork length; today they measure *total* length. Thus, today's 50-incher is 1½ inches shorter than would have been a 50-incher measured a generation ago.

Total Length (inches)	Weight (pounds)	Age (years)
12	½	2
16	1½	3
18–20	2½	4
21–22	4	5
23–25	5	6
27	6½	7
29–32	9	8
35	15	9
39	18	10–12
40–49	28–45	14+
48	42+	16+
50	45–50	18+
50–53	49+	20+

The size and age chart above is a highly approximated average of striper lengths, weights, and ages of such fish. Individual variations caused by season, river of origin, and sex make this an educated approximation. These numbers are *total* length and reflect today's system of measurement. When combined with the young-of-the-year index, it is possible to predict the size opportunities of striper fishing for a given year.

FIFTY—THE MAGIC MARK

I am not certain how the tradition began, but the most acclaimed measure of a trophy striper is that of 50 pounds. In our topsy-turvy world of exaggeration, braggadocio, and fragile egos, you may as well catch a schoolie if all you are going to catch is a 49-pounder. When I was a weighmaster, guys used to break their toes kicking the tires of their buggy when it happened—my wife, Joyce, one of them. Maybe 50 pounds was a milestone that combined the right quantities of rarity and possibility. Tackle companies have given awards for that size, as with the old Ashaway Line and Twine's "Nifty Fifty Club." For years the Schaefer Brewery in New York also gave awards for such fish. And the traditional point at which most striper piscophiles run to the taxidermist is 50 pounds.

The greatest known total of 50s was around 225 in one season in the late 1960s. In 1966, 125 were reported, both years about 10 percent taken from the surf. Just prior to when the fishery crashed, there was a historically important season in 1981 during which more 50-pounders were caught than ever before. However, the brewery that had once maintained such records, having been criticized for rewarding the slaughter of our biggest stripers, had stopped awarding and stopped counting. So no one knows exactly how many monsters were taken during what was perhaps the biggest year in striper-fishing history. Examining old records of some of the striper clubs of the time,

The most acclaimed measure of a trophy striper is that of 50 pounds.

top club fish varied from 42 to 45 pounds in the early 1960s. You could almost see them grow, similar to what we are experiencing today.

At any rate, for surfcasters, 50-pounders don't come easily. The golden mark of 50 pounds has always seemed silly to me. A good fish should have been mounted anyway. An outrageous number of very competent anglers, both surf and boat fishing, have never taken a "fifty," and many of those who have were just lucky, nothing more. Moreover, I have seen such fish corrupt surfcasters into believing that they possessed some God-given talent after catching one. Followed by years of frustration, they usually end up boat fishing and still never see another. Fly fishing? The two over 50 pounds in the fly-fishing world records were apparently taken in boats in Oregon's Smith River. No one knows how many people fish for stripers in the Northwest Atlantic. Divide up a hundred 50-pounders, the yield of such fish in a good year, among those of us out there, and there are bound to be millions of disappointed anglers.

There are no formally kept records for *surf*-caught stripers. Even fly-fishing records for bass make no distinction between surf- and boat-caught record fish. There is the all-tackle listing and the fly-fishing category.

TIME AND WEIGHT LOSS

Everyone recognizes that fish lose weight out of the water. Still, the extent of this weight loss is perhaps the most exaggerated aspect in the shaky technology of fish measurement, and stripers are no exception. There has been some amateur science in this regard, and those who have sought to determine a rate of dehydration commonly agree at 0.5 to 1 percent—4 to 8 ounces—the first day. After that, dehydration—if it can be measured at all—drops off markedly. The recommended procedure is to weigh the fish as soon as possible and make no allowances for dehydration. However, I have heard of some with a huge striper who have stored it in a bathtub (their wives must have loved that). Others have put the fish under a wet towel in a bed of ice until a weigh station opened. The issue of weight loss with time gets plenty of attention because occasionally, especially years when there are concentrations of a certain size of fish—coupled with competition, which in itself has been known to corrupt anglers—an ounce here or there can make the difference. It is something fishers believe they can affect.

Sealed scales might be required by the IGFA, but bragging rights are informal, and being able to say you caught a certain size of fish is not something that many tackle shops take seriously. (Maybe they know something about us.) Profits can be sparse in some of these places, and having an accurate digitized scale is not always a priority—polite-speak for saying if you weigh it often enough, you may be able to get pretty much what you want.

KEEPERS

The term *keeper* is a postmoratorium (late 1980s on) term that was born from the repeated raising of the size limit for the allowable "reduction to possession" of a striper. Keepers had little importance in the old days because, here in the North, few migration-capable bass were throwbacks what with a size limit of 16 inches. Recent attention to the term is a natural outgrowth of the continuous contaction of fish up to 18 pounds not suitably legal during some years of the restoration. Also, there is—depending upon what years you are speaking of—great variations in "keepers." With 36-inch fish weighing 18-ish pounds and 28-inch fish weighing half that, both keepers depending upon the year, there is little definition of size to be derived from the term in spite of the logic of its development and use. At this writing some striper states have "keepers" that are 24 inches, weighing less than 5 pounds. For convenience, the next level of striper in need of definition would be the trophy, which, while lacking a clear definition, could be considered a size larger than what is commonly caught. Today's trophy will be tomorrow's routine encounter, probably until fair numbers of 50-pounders are available.

STOCK IDENTIFICATION

Because all stripers appear the same, it is difficult to determine river of origin—what biologists call stock identification. It is important to know what percentage of the stripers in our fore come from what source or stock composition. DNA science makes this determination possible, but no such project, at this writing, has yet been undertaken in modern times to determine what percentages of migratory stripers from a particular source are of the total. Old studies indicated that 90 percent of stocks were southern, 9 percent were Hudson, and 1 percent all others; no doubt there are some shifts in stock composition, as the various fecundity rates of some races vary. We can expect great or small numbers from a particular river's year-class, but the wild card will always be that anomaly fish originating from a river during a "bad" year. Thus, while what most of us are catching is governed by what we think was born, now and then someone catches a monster from a bad year or from a less renowned river; this happens just often enough to keep us on our toes and to remind us about how little we understand. It is a big ocean, and its secrets are well kept.

INCHES DON'T DEFINE

Many of the size discussions about stripers now utilize inches as opposed to pounds. This is a direct result of ten years of preoccupation with fish that had to be measured. Of course it is understandable, because how else is a person to determine a lineside's qualifications without hurting it while being pushed and bullied by a raging surf in the deep night? Thus, while inches may work, length is a poor measure of a striper's size. It should, in my opinion, be pounds—the traditional measure—because individual conditions can create dramatic differences between two stripers of the same length. Using a sixteen-year-old year-class as an example, a 42-inch fish could be as heavy as 38 pounds or as light as 28. Contemporary measurement might call this a tie, but I say that somebody has lost the competition by 10 pounds. Again, what seems to corrupt many of us is what we want to believe about a fish that we have released. The so-called BogaGrip is a nice way to both handle and weigh a live struggling bass—one more item for the backpack.

INDIVIDUAL CONDITION

As with mammals, individual condition will define much of the striper's potential in terms of being able to resist, to fight. Thin fish, athletic ones that carry less weight but the same muscle, can put up enough fight to the rod to fool anglers into believing that they have latched onto something much bigger. Such "racers," as they are called, are famous for making experienced surf fishers beg for help in the surf or retch in the dunes if they've dropped them or broken off. Still, don't buy into the notion that long, thin "racers" are males. They are just thin anomalies among the species. Some old-timers still refer to outsized bass as bull bass, although they are really cows, and even those knowing better continue to use the term. Because half are males, all the conservation practices in the world deny half of all that is born from ever being outsized. When you take this into account, even if there were never a line or net thrown, all males of a year-class would be gone after eight years or so. Racers fight hard and win battles, not fishing contests.

Bass that have fed heartily will build up a higher-than-healthful amount of lactic acid in their blood. Analogous to that, they will also weigh more because of the bait in their digestive system. You will see more of this in fall, and the combination does not contribute to their ability to put up much resistance to the rod. Also, lactic acid builds more quickly in warm water, which is another of autumn's features.

WORLD-RECORD RICHES?

Many believe that either an all-tackle world record (or something close to that in size) will foster independent wealth or launch that person into a new career in the outdoors—perhaps retailing or guiding or garnering endorsements. Not so—case in point: Charles E. Cinto, who took the biggest lineside in over fifty years, got two reels, a case of plugs, and a week (without pay) appearing at a sporting show. The notion is somewhat controversial, but I believe that no grand accolades are likely to follow a person with an exceptional striped bass. The idea of exaggerated, overblown rewards has put a price on the head of our all-important gamefish. What a bounty on a great fish of any species does do is act as an incentive for someone to get into weighing shenanigans. In my lifetime on the Striper Coast I have seen plenty of games played, and all those games do is to give everybody something to talk about.

Stripers and the Freshwater Connection

Rock fights—a term used to describe the striper spawning ritual in southern spawning rivers—take place late spring in fresh water that is barely deep enough to cover a big female's back. This of course happens largely at night because the linesides require the cover of darkness in such shallow water or they would be vulnerable to every protein-consuming animal in the territory. From the moment of fertilization, juvenile bass are way upriver in sweet water, and they stay there until weeks later before dropping down into the salt chuck. It is classic anadromous—saltwater fish spawning in fresh—behavior. All through this discussion, you will see that this aspect of their natural history, the affinity to fresh water, will prove to be important.

If they could, striped bass would visit fresh water much more often than simply when ripe with spawn, but the dams on our more *important* rivers prevent that. Examples abound of rivers that stop stripers from spreading their population to other valleys—a shame, really, or we might walk a river, bank to bank, on their backs the way historical accounts say that the colonists did.

The first time I was given insight into stripers' freshwater affinity was when I investigated the fish elevator in Holyoke, Massachusetts, for an *Outdoor Life* assignment. Thousands of shad, eels, trout, sturgeon—you name it—were being lifted along with occasional stripers that were found as far upriver as Turners Falls. All species were looking to climb higher into the freshwater source, nearly 100 miles from the ocean. Except for eels, which are catadromous—and thus going "home" to sweet water—all the other species were anadromous. Yet of them all, the stripers were the most rare because back then, twenty years ago, it was unusual for a lineside to make it over the next downstream obstruction, Enfield Dam. Still, the years have been kinder to the river than to Enfield Dam, as it has deteriorated so markedly that everything, including stripers, is scooting past the tumbled-down, rock-studded obstacle so that striper fishing below Holyoke Dam, the next upriver obstruction, is memorable in June. They say that bass are there because they have followed the scent of alewives. I don't know how true that is, but I do know that sweet water is not foreign to them and they would probably go there just for the trip. They have done so for centuries everywhere else.

A similar situation is apparent on the Hudson River only 65 air miles west. Some stripers get over the Troy Dam there during periods of high water, be they unusual tides or runoff snowmelt from the spring freshet. Locks, which are used by boat traffic to get over the dam, are more likely the means, if any, that stripers have for getting upriver. Otherwise the dam is an obstacle that bars the movement of river fish, upsetting the natural tendency of free-moving species from salt water to fresh. Were stripers, or their forage—which also runs the river—allowed to pass, we would not need to rely upon only a handful of rivers for our coastal fishery. Most of our major rivers in the Northeast could produce nearly as many as the Hudson, which, when combined, could match it in striper production. That may have been the case before the Industrial Revolution.

Since the striper restoration all through the 1990s, the Merrimack River north of Boston has often hosted great numbers of huge linesides. Area people in the know have been cashing in on it from late May, when big bass arrive north, until the end of June when alewives are finished dropping down from their own spawning run. The theory, and I would not dare argue with its logic, is that bass are there for the "herring" and leave when the herring depart. Makes sense. Big stripers mill below the Essex Dam in Lawrence without ever trying to mount the dam. They catch some corkers there, and nary a grain of salt is in the grog the many miles above the tide.

When we used to fish for Atlantic salmon on Maine's Penobscot River during the striper moratorium, somebody was always hooking up in one of the salmon pools, yelling like the dickens with sweaty "fish-ons" and begging for leave for a fierce downriver chase and "salmon" battle. The rest of us would politely step back from the riverbank to permit passage and pursuit, a thing all salmoneers learn to do if they don't want questions about their lineage. Invariably, that person, having spent a fortune in lodging, tags, designer clothes, and signature tackle, would express no small discontent and embarrassment over a "flippin' striper." Like its sister river the Merrimack, the Penobscot does also striper up at salmon time, but the Veazie Dam above Bangor shortens the trip.

Once you understand the psyche of Maine salmonid worship, with all its inherent trout and salmon traditions, you can't contemplate what happened to them on the Kennebec without a smile if you come from Massachusetts, or a polite cough if you come from Maine.

There has been a successful and exciting restoration of stripers in Maine's Kennebec River where, through the efforts of volunteers seeking brood stock stripers from federal sources, breeding populations have been reestablished. The Edwards Dam in Augusta has been an impediment to the river's relationship to the Atlantic for all too long. Few of the species that were once found in the Kennebec remain, and those that do are a mere semblance of what they were. Salmon, stripers, sturgeon, and alewives, all ingredients found in the anadromous mix that are rapidly dying off, milled aimlessly in the shadow of Edwards Dam unable to complete the cycle founded in antiquity. Historical accounts dating back to the late 1700s—before the dam's construction in 1837—mention "a thousand stripers in a single weir." Highly organized, dedicated conservationists like American Rivers, Natural Resources Council of Maine, Trout Unlimited, and the Atlantic Salmon Federation fought to have the dam breached to open this significant stream, which finds its source on the Canadian border. Their success in doing this July 1999 is one of the prime conservation stories of our time. These miles are suitable for angling, but it is not yet known what contribution this stretch makes to spawning.

What no one ever anticipated was that once access to the river was attained by "sea-runs," significant numbers of stripers would run the Kennebec clear to Waterville—an upriver location 17 miles past Augusta, where few had ever even heard of striped bass—to feed on trout and landlocked salmon. Mainers will mumble when coyotes eat their deer, and they might resent the disappearance of house pets for the same reason because in their hearts it is viewed as natural; however, stripers sacrilegiously predating on their trout and salmon is going way over the line. Give striped bass a river and they will go.

Different from the others because this time it was not a dam that obstructed the river but pollution in Philadelphia, the Delaware River has been cleaned up enough there for the passage of sea-run stripers to their traditional spawning grounds. Previously the Philadelphia tidewater was so polluted that it lacked suitable oxygen to support bass as well as other fish, and indigenous species could not make it through to traditional spawning beds. Today big bass are commonly taken during the spring spawn 300 miles from the Atlantic above Phillipsburg, New Jersey. The present New Jersey freshwater record of 36 pounds, 8 ounces was taken here, as was the former record of 35 pounds. Moreover, now that the low-oxygen barrier of Philadelphia is no longer an issue, the upstream migration limits are nearly boundless.

It's easy to conjure up an image of a Catskills trout fisher having a trout on and gasping at seeing it inhaled by a moby striper. When I asked well-known Delaware River guide Kevin Riley if he knew of this happening and if so how far upriver, he came back with an animated response that reflected his own river experience.

Kevin Riley wrote:

As a free flowing river from its tail waters to the ocean, the Delaware gets most of its flow from the east and west branches which meet at Hancock. Good years, stripers will travel into the upper branches 17 and 33 miles north of Hancock respectively to Cannonsville and Pepacton Reservoirs, 340 to 370 miles from the ocean. I'm sure that some of these brutes make their way to these tail waters because there is nothing to stop them from where we routinely see them at Hancock's Junction Pool, the point where the east and west branches meet to form the Upper Delaware. Trout fishers, fly fishing for wild browns and rainbows, have been known to take stripers on their big streamer patterns by accident while trout fishing. Also, on quite a few occasions, while reeling in a smallmouth, we have had stripers follow it to the boat. Smallmouth, trout, sunfish, it doesn't matter if a striper is hungry it will eat an easy meal. A few seasons ago I had a smallie on (I saw it jump) when all of a sudden my line took off downriver when a striper took the smallie that I had caught on a Rapala. I wound up catching a 26-inch striper instead of the 12-inch bass I started with! So it does happen not only to fly fishermen, but to spin anglers too. Depicting a trout fisher being surprised by a striper would not be stretching the truth by any means. It happens.

Thanks, Kevin.

Striper populations in our Northwest Atlantic are at a level greater than any known in living memory, and rising. True, much is attributable to Maryland and Virginia record juvenile indices. Further, "new" contributing rivers are joining the list. Just what a higher number of natal striper rivers will mean to the fishery is a wild card at this point, but the prognosis for "wild fish" has never been better.

Domestication of Stripers

Farming of striped bass is in its infancy, but what work has been done in raising the species indicates that they are not difficult to rear commercially in hatcheries. Our U.S. Fish and Wildlife Service produced eleven million juvenile bass during the 1990s restoration effort. Even today, there is no evidence of what part of our present robust return has been the product of that stocking. What is known—through coded wire implant tags—is that domestic stock-outs have done well.

Some scientific observers are convinced that we have strains of superbass among our wild stocks, known as "contingents," which exhibit superior growth characteristics not representative of the population at large. (Is that Alfred Hitchcock music in the background?) If stock identification could be refined through DNA science, would it not be possible to identify and then isolate such "families" of better-growing striped bass for cultivation? Of course all this is academic when we already have more bass than anyone alive has ever seen.

Blues in the Striper Surf

Over the years there has been some evidence that populations of bluefish and stripers are inversely proportional. Any number of times when striper numbers were down, the blues happened to be at a high point in their population. The term *cyclical* is often used to describe the variations in both their numbers, but that is not quite accurate because there is no purity in the rise and fall in their populations. The latest example of population relationships was in the 1970s when bass numbers plummeted, and so many blues were in our Northwest Atlantic that they were seen in Maine for the first time in a hundred years. With most marine species, it is not until numbers peak that they stretch their normal range, which was the case then. At this writing bluefish seem to be in good numbers, and bass are in evidence more than anytime in my life. The theory, therefore, is not holding true in this case. More junk science, which will not be the first time we've seen it in the striper surf.

Blues are to striper fishing what bluegills are to perch fishing, and what pickerel are to bass fishing. Often utilizing the same forage, they come together incidentally in the striper surf, and most water that supports stripers will sooner or later host bluefish. Invariably, the shore fisher is going to encounter bluefish on a regular basis, because they are part of surf fishing for stripers. Some purists might cringe at the notion of toothed marauders darting and sliding through the first wave toward their finely crafted flies, but blues have saved many nights of fly casting when bass were unavailable. And while there might be some controversy over their place in this book, I think they play a major role in the fun and frolic of striper fishing in general and fly fishing in particular. Why not? Fishing is bad one night and you hook up suddenly and it happens to be a bluefish. They are a bonus.

For that minority of us who happen to like eating blues, they are something to bring home for the table. They enjoy liberal regulation with no current size limit and a bag limit of ten—nine more than I can eat. I would prefer eating small, fresh bluefish, when fried in butter or grilled in a bath of mayo, to eating striped bass. We had better get back to fishing before I salivate all over my keyboard.

Anyone with a modicum of beach-fishing experience is aware of blues' reputation for fighting, pound for pound, way better than

Bluefish can be stand-ins for stripers and have saved many nights of fishing.

stripers. My best blue on a fly is 16 pounds; with surfcasting gear, 18. When assigning fight-meter values, I would attribute their ability to impart force at a rate of two to one: A 10-pound blue is equal to a 20-pound striper. Blues will also jump much more than stripers, and they will go much deeper into your backing. The teeth of bluefish present a special set of problems.

Plug fishers can sometimes get away without using a wire leader; the fly, on the other hand, is more easily engulfed on the take. Consequently, you are going to lose flies to bluefish if you are caught unaware some night while striper fishing. Commonly you will "break off" without realizing that you were cut off. Sometimes they will snip the leader so quickly, without applying any force to your equipment, that you do not even know your fly is gone. What is more distressing than fishing an empty leader? Naturally, the answer is to fish with a fine-wire leader, but wire usually interferes with striper takes, which is a lesson learned with all other options used on stripers. The solution is to stay with a mono tippet and take your chances. I have found that if you do, slightly less than half the time the blue will bite through the leader, the rate of cutoffs increasing with bluefish size. What does rule in our favor is that blues, unlike stripers, which are headhunters, bite or take from behind. Therefore, it is possible to dress flies on longer-shank hooks and have the use of some tooth protection. My fly wallet has a special page for bluefish.

You don't want to crimp wire to a fly because it causes the connection to hinge unnaturally. What I do is form a loop after passing the wire though the hook eye before even dressing the fly with the loop crimped closed around the shank. Then I pin it down on the body with nylon so that the wire protrudes for, say, 2 inches, with a very small loop at the tippet end of the wire. It is not a nice presentation, but I dislike leaving bluefish in the water with a fly in them. There is no defense from some hazards.

When the water is so loaded with blues that they are roughing the surface like oil sizzling, it is dangerous to cast. The more there are, the more competitive and frenzied they can get. If you happen to have just one little weed get on your fly line, and it moves as a consequence of your stripping or even from a legitimate hit, another bluefish is going to hit the weed. Thinking it to be something alive, the blue is going to damage your fly line or cut it cleanly.

Many experienced surfcasters believe that bluefish are the fools of the Striper Coast in the sense that they will take anything thrown at them. The species does not enjoy the respect that it deserves, because I have seen them exhibit selective behavior at times. Once after a night of fishing, I was driving off the beach when I saw a bunch of slicks the size of patio tables spread at random in the flat calm of a developing dawn. Thinking this situation a cinch, I put out a big popping plug that I was certain would bring them up—nothing. Then, remembering that I had eels left over, I decided to put one out just to see if the reasons for the slicks were still around. I couldn't get the eel back, unless you count 2-inch cigars wriggling on the hook.

Arrivals and departures are different from those of stripers. Blues are not a springtime species, and some parts of the northern Striper Coast do not see them until August. Blues can linger well into the winter, however, because of the water temperature's tendency to fall slowly. We generally like to think that they leave before stripers, and it is said that as long as you are catching bluefish, striper fishing is not over, even if that is said during a snowstorm.

Blues enjoy a more worldwide range. In addition to being found throughout our East Coast over a much wider area than that of

When you a hook a bluefish like this one, be ready for a fight.

stripers, they are commonly taken in Australian waters and along the West African coast as far north as the Azores. Lieutenant Commander Henry Lyman, now publisher emeritus for *Salt Water Sportsman Magazine* and author of *Bluefishing* and other books, reported that, around World War II, he saw a bluefish that had been taken off the northwest African coast that weighed 45 pounds. A 24-pound all-tackle world record held for many years in the Azores before being replaced by a Carolinas 31-pound, 12-ounce behemoth. Only during years when bluefish populations peak do they stretch their range as far north as Maine. When blues first showed there in the 1970s, they had not been seen in a hundred years. Wherever they can be found, a fish approaching 20 pounds is a good one. You will see your backing when fighting specimens weighing way short of 20 pounds.

World Records

The following world records, courtesy of the IGFA, are as of late 2003 and are always subject to change, particularly in the fly-fishing category because of increasing interest in the method.

Utilizing the same forage, blues and stripers come together incidentally in the striper surf. Most water that supports stripers will sooner or later host bluefish.

MEN'S STRIPED BASS FLY-FISHING WORLD RECORDS
(Courtesy: International Game Fish Association)

Tippet Class	Weight	Catch Place	Catch Date	Angler
2 lb.	14 lb., 4 oz.	Chesapeake Bay, VA	11/13/00	Mike Marsala
4 lb.	19 lb., 8 oz.	Misquamicut, RI	8/6/97	Alan Caolo
6 lb.	24 lb., 12 oz.	American River, CA	12/2/73	Alfred Perryman
8 lb.	42 lb.	Sacramento River, CA	5/30/86	R. S. Hayashi
12 lb.	64 lb., 8 oz.	Smith River, OR	7/28/73	Beryl E. Bliss
16 lb.	51 lb., 8 oz.	Smith River, OR	5/18/74	Gary L. Dyer
20 lb.	36 lb., 6 oz.	Raritan Bay, NJ	4/24/02	Richard A. Fink

WOMEN'S STRIPED BASS FLY-FISHING WORLD RECORDS
(Courtesy: International Game Fish Association)

Tippet Class	Weight	Catch Place	Catch Date	Angler
2 lb.	2 lb., 12 oz.	Chesapeake Bay, VA	10/29/99	Emily G. Rountrey
4 lb.	9 lb.	Chatham, MA	7/11/02	Donna E. Anderson
6 lb.	24 lb.	Oregon Inlet, NC	1/27/02	Mrs. S. R. Hutchins
8 lb.	20 lb.	Oregon Inlet, NC	1/27/02	Mrs. S. R. Hutchins
12 lb.	27 lb., 8 oz.	Oregon Inlet, NC	1/27/02	Mrs. S. R. Hutchins
16 lb.	21 lb., 8 oz.	Oregon Inlet, NC	1/27/02	Mrs. S. R. Hutchins
20 lb.	21 lb., 8 oz.	Oregon Inlet, NC	12/23/01	Mrs. S. R. Hutchins

IGFA MEN'S LINE CLASS WORLD RECORDS (NON-FLY-FISHING)

(Courtesy: International Game Fish Association)

Line Class	Weight	Catch Place	Catch Date	Angler
2 lb.	21 lb.	San Francisco Bay, CA	1/20/92	Kirk E. Campbell
4 lb.	40 lb., 8 oz.	Cape Cod Bay, MA	5/25/85	Christoopher Van Duzer
6 lb.	56 lb., 14 oz.	Gay Head, MA	10/15/81	Richard C.Landon
8 lb.	41 lb., 8 oz.	Fisher's Island, NY	8/27/95	Alan Golinski
12 lb.	66 lb., 12 oz.	Bradley Beach, NJ	11/1/79	Steven R. Thomas
16 lb.	69 lb.	Sandy Hook, NJ	11/18/82	Thomas James Russell
20 lb.	78 lb., 8 oz.	Atlantic City, NJ	9/21/82	Albert R. McReynolds
30 lb.	71 lb.	Norwalk, CT	7/14/80	John Baldino
50 lb.	76 lb.	Montauk, L. I., NY	7/17/81	Robert A. Rocchetta
80 lb.	70 lb.	Orient Point, NY	9/5/87	Chester A. Berry

IGFA WOMEN'S LINE CLASS WORLD RECORDS (NON-FLY-FISHING)

(Courtesy: International Game Fish Association)

Line Class	Weight	Catch Place	Catch Date	Angler
2 lb.	16 lb., 6 oz.	Rye, NH	7/21/99	Deborah A. Morrison
4 lb.	30 lb., 6 oz.	Cape Cod Bay, MA	5/24/85	Sharyn Guggino
6 lb.	46 lb., 12 oz.	Fishers Island, NY	9/4/95	Emme Golinski
8 lb.	40 lb., 2 oz.	Millicoma River, OR	4/5/85	Edna Skinner
12 lb.	48 lb., 9 oz.	Deal, NJ	7/27/80	Edna Yates
16 lb.	48 lb., 8 oz.	Monomoy Island, MA	7/16/91	Connie Codner
20 lb.	57 lb., 8 oz.	Block Island Sound, NY	8/28/59	Mary R. Aubry
30 lb.	64 lb., 8 oz.	North Truro, MA	8/14/60	Rosa O. Webb
50 lb.	64 lb.	Sea Bright, NJ	6/27/71	Mrs. Asie Espenak
80 lb.	57 lb., 4 oz.	Watch Hill, RI	8/24/97	Janice Masciarelli

8 Fifty Years of Fly Fishing

When I began to fly fish in 1948, I had a state-of-the-art cane Montague brook rod suffering from a gravity-inspired set and metal ferrules green from tarnish. I saved my muskrat-trapping money for one of those fancy newly invented solid glass rods. For flies I had some pet trees at the Blackstone Rod and Gun Club where the real fly fishermen left them; some of them were very nice. If there was no one around I would climb those trees, bend the branches without breaking them because they were needed to catch tomorrow's flies, and pluck some real fancy ones—Mickey Finns and other elegant creations used in faraway rivers.

The outflow from the club pond was Fox Brook, which was privately posted against fishing and where the owner stocked some very nice browns. Days when he was not patrolling it with his two Dobermans, you could let out line and dance a streamer or worm in the current and remain undetected. The brook trout were escapees from the club, and the browns belonged to the guy with the dogs. At the time there was only one other fly fisherman that I knew, Harry Beane, who was also twelve years old. He had all the stuff: a hat with flies on it, a wicker basket creel to put his fish in, and even a landing net, which was more sophisticated than dragging the trout up onto the bank the way I did. Release trout? Why would you want to do that? I believe Harry had the advantage of knowing more real trout fishermen than I, but he was always pleasant when we met fishing and when we did we would agree to each take a stretch of the posted part of Fox Brook so as not to interfere with one another.

After a couple of years of fishing the brook, I finally took some of my savings from trapping and joined the Rod and Gun Club so I could fish the club weekends. I had fished it for so long as a poacher

Fourteen-year-old Frank Daignault with an 18-inch rainbow trout taken in the bad-old days of trout fishing when a foot-long trout was a nice fish. Courtesy: *Woonsocket (R.I.) Call,* 1950.

that it took me almost two years to get used to fishing it with others. The club also had a piece of Fox Brook, roughly a tenth of a mile, running into the club's pond. I liked the brook because you didn't have to fly cast, something that I had not yet mastered. I used to see the accomplished fly fishermen roll the line a long way, but I could not yet do that. Then fly casting for me meant letting a lot of line out and having the current take it. My way of compensating was to stay in the brook. I learned quickly that trout had a propensity for upstream movement, and I caught more trout than most other members did by just fishing the brook.

One Saturday, when we had just stocked and some of the gang was fishing there, an older member, maybe forty years old, told me that he had a fly line for me.

"This line is a little worn," he said, "but it's tapered and will still cast better than the one you have."

I had always wondered why people used those expensive fly lines. To me you could get a level fly line for the price of two muskrats while one of those fancy ones cost the value of five. It was too painful rolling up my sleeves to dip my arm in the brook in January to make muskrat sets to waste good trapping money on a fly line that exhibited no discernible results. Of course when you are fourteen the difference between a level and tapered fly line is kind of abstract and, unlike someone like Harry, I had little guidance in fly fishing because my father was a largemouth bass fisherman who was fond of lily pad edges.

It must have been around the same year (because I was still using my bike to go fishing) that I started seeing Bob Lipka. I first met him my second year in the first grade and we used to talk fishing all the time because we both lived biking distance from Horseshoe Falls. There had been a stocking of trout, and we had been really hot onto the fishing all weekend when we both decided to fish it in the morning before school on Monday. That day, if you stood on the bridge staring into the current, you could see the trout facing upstream. Bob and I got involved and didn't bother with school that morning. Around 10 AM my father walked out into the river with his glossy black fire department inspection shoes and dragged me out of the river for school.

Some years went by—school, military, girls, babies—and I met Bob Lipka again striper fishing. We ran into one another often at Narrow River or on Nauset Beach. By then, mid-1960s, he was running

Rip Tide Tackle in Woonsocket, Rhode Island, which was a specialty shop for fly fishermen. I had not seen Bob since we had drifted worms together at Horseshoe Falls or rope swung over Harris Pond.

"You fly fishing these things?"

"Been thinking about it."

"They're suckers for flies."

"I'll fix you up with something good, the whole rig, for a hundred."

He could see on my face that I thought a hundred dollars was a lot of money.

"Fifty bucks—rod, reel, and line, and I'll throw in some flies."

That night we went to a spot on the Cape's Pleasant Bay. Bobby shoved a fly rod into my hands, playing it down as though it was something that I had to do for him. The 50 feet of 10-weight fly line slid through the guides, settled on the bay surface, then drifted left, followed by a swirl.

"See that?" Bobby exclaimed.

After it swung a few more feet, I lifted the line and dropped the fly to the upcurrent right where it was inhaled by a brute, which made the placid waters of Pleasant Bay bulge, before it ran off into the reel's backing.

"Geezus!" Bobby yelled as he backed away. Then I reached for the reel, the handle dusting my knuckles, causing the line to lift higher before the leader broke.

"What happened?" Bobby asked.

"Shut up."

Trading use of the fly rod back and forth with me until dawn, Bobby rambled on about how the fly was so good for stripers that it should be banned, like they had done with nets. He said that I could have the use of it all week and that the fly rod—now down to a buck a week for a year—was the way to fish Scup Hole. Leaving our buggy in the gold glow of a new Cape Cod day, heading to town with my share of the night's bass, he called to me, as I dragged my weary body into our camper, "Keep the freakin' fly rod, butt face."

Until then I had thought that you had to be a little nuts to go fishing in the ocean with a fly rod. But like brothers we had lived the progression of going from trout to stripers, and when Bob Lipka said that fly fishing was a good thing for them, you just didn't question it. I knew he was competent and I trusted him.

In the ensuing years the fly rod occupied roughly 20 percent of my fishing in the striper surf. The reason for the small percentage of time was that we were rod-and-reel commercials, often fishing in crowds of other commercials, and begging leave on a red-hot tide rip with a fish on was not something the others would have honored more than once. Still, there were often times when the dainty, safe-looking little tuft of phony sand eel was all that they would take, and our buggy never went anywhere without that 9-footer on the roof because we were both—fly rod and I—veterans of Fox Brook, of Harry and Bob.

When we lost stripers, we fished for anything that might replace our lost adventure. 1983 photo.

In the early 1980s, after a couple of halcyon years of big bass and few small ones, the striped bass population of the Northwest Atlantic crashed to all-time lows. Life became difficult without the adventure we had once known in the striper surf. It was so bad, so distressing, that we turned to some of the more glamorous freshwater pursuits, because life is too short not to keep looking for challenging experiences.

In Pulaski, New York, on the east bank of Lake Ontario where tributary streams flow west, steelhead run the rivers beginning in November and keep at it until April. Unlike the Pacific salmon there in early fall, the steelhead take handily, fight well, grow bigger than blue-

Lake Ontario steelhead kept us busy winters.

fish, and are fished in forested hills where streams babble their way to the lake. Steelheading Lake Ontario tributary streams is a little like Fox Brook, a lot like Horseshoe Falls, and as exciting as big stripers on the beach; only there you fight them in the woods, and in the snow. This topsy-turvy world of flow-dependent rivers often presented some unique sets of conditions that, while a riddle at first, made sense after a while. For instance, river fishers would pray for a warm day to fish in—then the snowmelt that resulted from such warmth would inundate the banks with flood and cold water. Cold days the water was warm because there was no melting ice to contribute to the river. If it was too cold, slush ice stopped the fishing. Nevertheless, if you had learned trout fishing in the bad-old days, where a 15-incher was a monster, a 15-pounder was a memorable trophy, and we caught quite a few of that size. A 10-pound rainbow was average, and we knew of no one who would walk 20 feet to see one.

Around the same time, early 1980s, Massachusetts tried to develop their sea-run trout program, which was largely directed to small Cape Cod streams. A put, grow, and take fishery, these little brooks with direct access to the salt were stocked with year-old 7-inch browns that went down into local tidewater without migrating, returning a year later at 15 inches and two years later at trophy size. While in their "natal" rivers, the rivers where they had been stocked, they were usually on a spawning run—often on a redd—and little interested in taking a fly. Sure, some fish were taken, especially nice second-year fish, but they were still safe because most of the trout types did not believe in killing a fish.

These browns were a marvelous study in coloration. If you were lucky enough to take a sea-run that had come up very recently, it was a silver-bodied specimen with a dark chocolate-brown back. If you caught a male in full spawning colors, it was adorned with a dark brown back, mustard-yellow flanks, and festooned with red or blue dots with yellow halos. The danger in having one in your hands was that you might look at it too long. The charm for me of fishing for these novelty trout was fishing them in tidewater because they were symbolic of my two favorite kinds of fly fishing.

When your formative years were spent at Fox Brook, there was something almost surreal about trout fishing in the salt chuck. You really didn't believe it until you caught a trout in tidewater. If you think about it, there are many parts of the world, such as Norway and the British Isles, where wild trout run from the sea. It was just amazing.

I had a favorite pool in an estuary to the Cape's Waquoit Bay where I could sometimes watch the baitfish sprinkle along the eelgrass as though a bluefish were cruising there. Often, as the tide formed up, browns, some none too shabby, would take position facing the current. But, ah, they were browns, and you don't know selectivity until you have fished for mature browns. (Striped bass are dummies by comparison.) I have forgotten who said it, where I learned it, or even if it was true, but I got the idea somewhere that they often foraged on leeches. I went begging to Harry, who by now was a grandfather himself and had never—even when we were kids—resorted to getting his flies from the trees. Harry showed me how to tie a leech, a bushy, buggy-looking black one, out of black marabou.

One day, late January, a day when only a fool would go trout fishing in the ocean a hundred miles from home on a day trip, I saw the biggest trout this side of Pulaski take up position in one of my tidewater pools. When I went to fish for him with my leech he disappeared, where I didn't know. Half an hour later I was waiting for my sinking line to settle deeper, started my retrieve, and saw a white mouth open in the depths of the pool. I could not help but think . . . hope this white mouth was opening for my leech. It was, and I was fast to the biggest trout in Massachusetts. Leaving the depth of the pool, the behemoth tore line from my drag toward the eelgrass. Wading out onto the shallow flats on the side of the pool, I chased it with my net, gave up some line, chased it some more, took in some line, and netted it like a starving caveman. For a 4-pound tippet, 7 pounds is a nice trout, a nice wild trout.

With stripers gone, talk of a moratorium where no fish would be taken, commercial fishing closed down in a fishery where there were not enough fish to be skunked on, ours was a continuing search for more adventure—this time Atlantic salmon.

Maine was working with a native strain of salmon from a local river, the Narraguagis. The idea with salmon was to have a genetically suitable strain of salmon that could withstand the rigors of local climate. With federal assistance, the Maine Sea-Run Salmon Commission reared a million juvenile salmon for stocking into the Penobscot River in Bangor. On average their return was 0.5 percent, but five thousand

Summers we traveled through Maine for landlocked
salmon like this one for Joyce. 1984 photo.

salmon, having started with a million, can be good fishing, especially
when the Veazie Dam stops them from going upriver and they lie in
pools wondering if they will ever find the fish ladder or elevator. *Pools*
makes it sound easy, like the fish are confined, but it isn't, because they
are unrestricted and they can go anywhere.

The Atlantic salmon is not like a striped bass that is going to want
your fly because it looks like a sand eel or a shrimp. Salmon are in the
river to party and they do not eat at this time. Sure, some distant
memory of its pre-smolt life might spirit one long enough to instinc-

tively pull your fly down. One in a thousand will do that, which leaves 4,995 others laughing at your efforts. Of course, if you have ever fished for Atlantic salmon—and you poor bugger, what are you living for if you haven't—getting an impossible fish to take is the whole game. It is just harder to understand when you are a striper fisherman. Until I got to Maine, I thought being a striper fisherman was an advantage.

Having been a Cape Cod fly fisher in a world where no one fly fished, I had never had the opportunity to know what genuine fly fishers did. When you spent your formative years hiding from Dobermans on posted land with a level line, your methods were kind of undeveloped, sort of isolated, and distinctly primitive. Maine salmoneers were serious, out for blood. Worse, they knew how to cast and had tapered lines to do it. To add insult to injury, while they didn't need them, they cheated and used shooting heads, which dumped a line farther than I could throw a tin with a squidder. They even utilized special knots that presented the fly so that it performed under tension, an aptitude I don't have to this day.

Naturally, when I tied a fly on, I utilized the same knot as in striper fishing—a simple clinch knot. There was no reason to change, because I caught as many salmon as everybody else did, which doesn't say much, as few salmon really took a fly. Then one morning a guy sitting on one of the benches where the most salmon fishing took place reminded me that "this is not a riffling river." And I, wanting neither to be embarrassed nor to divulge my ignorance about salmon fishing, shrugged and kind of let it slide. A season later, a different salmon fisher asked me if I did well "riffling," which I thought was either something dirty or illegal. Because it bothered me, I asked him about it.

"Riffling is when you attach your fly so that it will ride on the top, the way you do."

Next pass through the pool, maybe an hour later, sonovagun didn't my fly actually skim across the surface of the river. Then it hit me all at once why a Cape Cod "flatlandah" could come to Maine and not only do as well as everybody else, but many days actually do better. That season I had a morning when I landed five salmon from 8 to 16 pounds when twenty others—who really knew how to cast—beached three. By then I had learned from reading a book that you could put an overhand knot around the throat of your fly, then lock it down with another overhand. No longer riffling by accident, the fly skimmed the surface leaving a wake that was more pronounced. What those guys would have given to know about my little secret, because, after having spent a few years with them, I am certain they would bait a hook with anything they had two of in order to catch a salmon. It was that bad.

One morning, Dave Spencer, a local who was like that, showed up just off Wringer Pool in his boat in the predawn time when the river was alive with hopeful anglers. In Maine, where all rules were formulated out of convenience for the resident population of anglers, it was perfectly legal to place your boat right in the middle of a pool where everyone wanted to fish. My wife, Joyce, whose view of salmon fishing was to stone all landings and sell them to a fish market, having not so long ago fished for stripers, happened to grace us that day with her overwhelming Catholic presence. So as to force the cleansing of salmon-fishing vulgarities, she was sent through Wringer Pool first because there was nothing rolling anyway. I was close behind her, because all Joyce needs for a backcast is about 25 feet, and I saw her salmon's molars when it came up. It was classic salmon take: a head-and-tail dog roll that tightened her line, causing her to look back at me saying, "I think it's a perch."

"Set!" I shouted, not wanting her to lose what stood a good chance of being all she would contact that day, if not the whole trip.

Meanwhile, Spencer—because he had spent the night in fear of oversleeping his alarm, afraid that another boat fisher would take the spot he was abusing from us if he didn't get there with the owls—was sound asleep in the stern of his canoe. His leg was wrapped around his salmon pole, the fly dragging harmlessly in the current. In perfect salmon form, Joyce's fish cartwheeled riverward, throwing water in Spencer's face while he sagged uncontrollably in deep narcoleptic bliss. Half shouting and half upsetting his canoe, he seemed to be trying to bolt toward the riverbank in terror. For him it had to be one of those bad dreams where you are running and not getting anywhere. He told me later that it was not until we trapped it in the shallows for removal and release that he really believed "a woman could catch a salmon."

Explaining to Joyce that the killing of a salmon, what with one tag per season, would deny her access to the river, I added that killing a salmon would soil our cooler with blood. I urged her to understand that it would take half an hour to clean it and another half hour to cook it; and that while salmon is good eating, who wants to eat salmon all week? "When do we get to kill one," she asked, "the last day?"

The salmon thing had begun to take a positive hold upon my mind. In 1982, a year when the Salmon Commission predicted a poor run because of earlier stocking problems, we decided to go to Quebec, where we assumed they had more salmon. Taking all the traditional striper gear out of the buggy, in late June we packed our fly rods and clothes and went on a northern trip. The first river we went to was a fall-run river where it was too early. The next one we went to was a spring river, but the water was too low. On the road one day, while driving east across the Gaspé Peninsula, I saw a sign that said 50, so I bumped up our speed a trifle. Why waste good fishing time? When we got stopped for speeding, I found out that the speed limit was 50 kilometers, not miles, per hour, so we got a ticket.

The river split at the Forks in Causapscal. The south-flowing branch was a sanctuary for the salmon, so you couldn't fish there. For the other branch you only needed a fishing license and salmon stamp. They did not require a daily permit, a paid right to fish for salmon, the reason being there were no salmon in that part of the river. Below the Forks for 10 miles or so, they sold daily permits for twenty dollars per day because the ones headed for the sanctuary might pass, and there was a star-alignment-chance that you could possibly catch one if it stopped to rest. If you found yourself desperate, you could consider frightening a bear off one.

The river was cut into sectors that were apparently graded by the traditional yield of the particular stretch. The sectors were priced according to their fishability, the ability to give up taking salmon. Thus salmon fishing, as in the rest of the world outside the United States, was a commodity priced at whatever the traffic would bear. The notion that salmon fishing was really for the rich took on meaning and acted as a reminder that Maine salmon fishing was so crowded because it was done in the only "free country" in the world that had Atlantic salmon.

The Forks Pool was popular because it was known to hold resting salmon that were readying for the sanctuary climb; below it were lots of falls and pools. There were several places along the way where salmoneers could watch and salivate, shouting encouragement to the fish as they bounded aimlessly at the white water only to be thrown back. Back at the pool there were benches on both banks where the Quebecois sat gazing at the river in the hope of seeing a salmon occasionally rise in the current. Probably Causapscal's nearest thing to an athletic event, there were many townies equipped not to fish but rather to watch as though they were fans at a contest of some sort. Should a salmon come up in one of those head-and-tail rises that they were famous for with a fisher working the pool, they all shouted, *"Garde la mouche, garde la mouche,"* which in French means "watch the fly." It was all kind of carnival, kind of Fenway center field, causing you to feel like a character in a play or a member of the team. Then it hit you that those sonsabitches were really rooting for the salmon.

In contrast, where the salmon could be caught downriver, where the pools they favored were in evidence, where everybody knew the fishing was good, and where you also needed an expensive guide to find out, those fishing rights were a hundred dollars a day. Below that, on the Matapedia, the Glen Ellen stretch, you could redial all day in early January for the privilege of having your name put into a hat. How much? If you had to ask, you soon learned, you couldn't afford it.

One day, while buying our twenty-bucks-per-day passes along with the other street people from the States, a man stood beside one of the scales at the ministry office. He had a salmon that weighed 46 pounds. I could only stare and think how much it looked like a striped bass. The bigness of this monster salmon brought me back to the striper surf and to what we had known. I had a cold sense of not belonging, feeling like I was somewhere that I did not want to be, fishing for something as doomed as the striped bass. I could not shake the notion that striper fishers, like salmon fishers, were some sort of anachronism, actors in a play that had closed down for lack of interest. Like striped bass, for those who fished them, there had to be salmon. Back to Maine.

We were in the tidewater section of the Penobscot below Veazie Dam. This was a big river, which was largely white with foam generated by water flow over the dam. There were times, usually late June to early July, when the daily salmon take was as good as some Icelandic rivers where they paid ten thousand dollars per rod week to fish. Just like life in the striper surf, I would wake up in the deep night disturbed by a dream that somebody was doing something on the

Penobscot without me. They never did. One morning, climbing down the riverbank to Wringer Pool around 1 AM, I was astounded to find the salmon rolling in all the same places as they did during the day. Grinning to myself, I started to wonder . . . *Can they see at night? Do they hit at night? Is it okay to fish at night?* When a fifty-year-old fisherman who has caught everything at night—trout, bass, bullheads, cod, bluefish, and stripers—has to wonder, we are all in trouble. Of course they will, and they did. Only this time, an hour after midnight, there was no waiting an hour and a half in a rotation to drift a fly past salmon so bored with seeing flies pass that they moved for a little

Atlantic salmon always took us into our backing. 1984 photo.

peace. Could the salmon fishing have been better because I didn't have to share the pool with others? Or was it better because all fish are more active at night? For me it was a simple case of doing what I had always done in the striper surf. The only issue, more an embarrassment than anything, was that it had taken so long for me to try it.

Around 1989 Maine abandoned the expensive Atlantic Salmon Restoration Program in favor of a self-sustaining fishery; its much smaller return ended in the closure of sportfishing for salmon. That same year, the Maryland young-of-the-year striper index produced the second finest reproductive results in the history of its measure-

When stripers reappeared on our coast, it was a sign that the moratorium might end. 1990 photo.

ment—twenty-six. After that striped bass enjoyed continuous strong indices years in succession, ending the moratorium with wildly reliable schoolie fishing where we watched one year-class after another come along to inhale our flies. It was, for us, the second reversal of fortunes for stripers, seemingly suggesting that if we could no longer have salmon we could go back to stripers. And we did.

Years on Maine and Maritime salmon rivers had been good for me. I learned what serious fly fishers did to cast a line—things like shooting heads, double hauls, mending the drift. My tour of duty had shown that the riffle hitch, while born in salmon fishing generations ago, was my ace-in-the-hole when it came to all fishing with a fly under tension. Even my trout fishing was often done on the surface with the hitch. Still, I could see that fishing inspired by the striper moratorium, efforts to fill the angling gap, fell by the wayside as the bass began to recover. There was no further need to work the streams I had gone back to when I could find an outflow in tidewater and see my backing every night that I fished. With striper fishing better after their recovery than I had ever seen it before, even the Lake Ontario tributary steelhead failed to light any fire in my angling, and we

Family traditions are passed. Our granddaughter Monica Cross crafts a fly.

drifted away from all the things that had been inspired by the loss of stripers. We had come full circle.

Having done it all, I know that my heart is where striped bass lurk. I am too committed to the sweet song of the high surf and its wild fish to ever go back to a Fox Brook or Horseshoe Falls. These, like my youthful relationships with Harry and Bob, set my course through all the stones in a road that took me to the beaches and tidal rivers with which I became enamored. Some nights I remember that the tide is right somewhere in my memory and I sleep fitfully as though some part of me had gone without the whole me.

Life in the striper surf had left its mark in our family, and the fly had played no small part. One daughter purchased a home on the Maine coast so that she could fly fish. Her twin bought a kit to teach herself fly tying, then taught what she could to her daughter, our granddaughter. Our son, Dick, who had learned to love it while his dad was in the midst of its discovery, took his fishing to Alaskan salmon rivers. Somehow, and it never mattered where, fly fishing the striper surf always seemed to be a celebration done under an ethereal orchestra playing the sweet song of the high surf.

Harpswell estuary, Maine, summer 2003. We are visiting at Sue's estatelike coastal home when it occurs to one of the kids that we should walk down the staircase to the shore to cast the rise hurrying through the narrows there. Everyone is aware that a rising tide brings stripers, and the lowering sun casts a dull, golden sailor's-delight glow on the seascape. We are a family doing what we learned a lifetime ago, all swishing line in harmonic effort for a drift into the making tide. Not that we are good, or that we even care if we are. What is important here, now, is that we are together doing what we do best, pursuing striped bass with whatever we think might work. This is Susan's show, as it is her river, and she knows it well. Walking among us in command presence, providing encouragement, uttering reminders of a best tide, she adds memories of some other night when they came through as though on cue from some divine signal. Our flies hit the lines of infusion hurrying inland, then straighten and swing while each of us silently hopes that just one bass will anoint the gathering, validate us as the striper fishers we have always been. Just one bass was all we wanted. It came. They always do.

Having done it all from rainbows to salmon, we knew that adventure for us was in the striper surf.

Index